Leading and Motivating Global Teams

Integrating Offshore Centers and the Head Office

T0382808

Leading and Motivating Global Teams

Integrating Offshore Centers and the Head Office

Vimal Kumar Khanna

CRC Press
Taylor & Francis Group
Boca Raton London New York

CRC Press is an imprint of the
Taylor & Francis Group, an **informa** business

AN AUERBACH BOOK

CRC Press
Taylor & Francis Group
6000 Broken Sound Parkway NW, Suite 300
Boca Raton, FL 33487-2742

First issued in paperback 2022

Version Date: 20172219

ISBN 13: 978-1-03-247684-1 (pbk)
ISBN 13: 978-1-4987-8474-0 (hbk)

DOI: 10.1201/9781315155647

**Visit the Taylor & Francis Web site at
http://www.taylorandfrancis.com**

**and the CRC Press Web site at
http://www.crcpress.com**

Contents

Acknowledgments

I would like to thank the book's editor, John Wyzalek, and all of the people at Taylor & Francis Group who worked tirelessly to ensure timely publication of this book. I sincerely appreciate the efforts of John Wyzalek in giving necessary guidance and support, providing valuable inputs, and taking timely actions throughout the process of publication, to ensure release of a high-quality book.

I would like to thank reviewer Ginger Levin for providing excellent review comments that helped significantly improve the content of the book and bring it to its current form.

I would also like to acknowledge the support of the people who helped me start the journey of publishing this book with Taylor & Francis Group.

- The journey started with the well-reputed management book author and speaker Alfonso Bucero suggesting Taylor & Francis Group as being a suitable publisher for the topic of my book. I would like to thank him for sharing many valuable inputs with me, based on his prior experience publishing with Taylor & Francis Group.
- I would like to thank my first contact in the Taylor & Francis Group, Kristine Mednansky, for her help and support in initiating the publishing process, which culminated in John Wyzalek becoming the editor of the book.

About the Author

Vimal Kumar Khanna is the Founder and Managing Director of mCalibre Technologies. He has over 31 years of industry experience and has won multiple international honors for his contributions to the management and technology domains. He is listed in *Marquis Who's Who in the World*. He is also Honorary Editor of *IEEE Communications*, the official global publication of the *IEEE Communications Society*.

His sole-authored papers have been published in leading global refereed journals, magazines, and conferences. He is a frequent speaker at Project Management Institute (PMI) Global Congresses—North America, EMEA, and APAC. He is an invited contributing author to PMI publications and has also acted as a source for multiple articles of *PM Network* magazine, the official global publication of the PMI. He has published in the complete gamut of management topics, such as suggesting innovative project management techniques for managing complex projects involving large teams, managing talent in offshore centers, achieving customer satisfaction in services projects, dealing with negative bosses and toxic workplace environments, managing challenges in leading and motivating small teams, people management skills for managers at various levels of organization hierarchy, etc.

He has held leadership roles in a range of global leading companies—product development companies, services companies, large multibillion dollar companies, Tier-1 VCs funded start-ups, etc. He has handled a range of activities in these companies in his long career, such as heading and running offshore centers, general management, project management of complex projects with large teams, people management, technical leadership, business development for winning services projects, budgeting, customer interaction, etc.

Chapter 1

Introduction

A large number of global companies are running Offshore Centers in distant countries. These companies have augmented their project teams in their global Head Office (HO) with the Offshore Center teams. The projects are distributed across the Offshore Center and HO, with the Offshore Center managers and HO managers leading the project teams to deliver on the project objectives.

Offshore Centers generally have quite strong and capable teams and have the potential to make even more significant contributions to their parent companies. However, Offshore Center teams are facing a number of challenges that are preventing them from delivering to their full potential and, hence, limiting their contribution to their parent companies.

This book describes various challenges being faced by Offshore Centers, deeply analyzes their root causes, and suggests techniques to be applied by the Offshore Center managers and HO managers to address these challenges. The book suggests a *holistic approach* to address these issues by specifying the actions to be taken by managers at all levels of the organizational hierarchy, ranging from first-level project managers to senior/executive management personnel.

The suggested techniques are supported by numerous Case Studies presented in the book. These Case Studies relate to Offshore Centers of global leading companies of various types and sizes, including large multibillion-dollar global giants, start-ups/small companies, product development companies, services companies, etc. Thus, Offshore Center managers and HO managers belonging to the whole gamut of company types and sizes will benefit from the book.

The suggested techniques will allow Offshore Center managers and HO managers to:

- Hire, retain, train, groom, lead, motivate, and manage Offshore Center teams effectively, to improve their skills, productivity, and growth
- Facilitate offloading of large core, complex, and high-value projects of the company to Offshore Centers
- Allow Offshore Centers to integrate with the HO to ensure success of globally distributed projects but still retain their local work culture, to meet the expectations and aspirations of the Offshore Center employees
- Facilitate growth of Offshore Center employees to global top positions of the company
- Allow the Offshore Center managers to get the requisite freedom and authority over their teams to deliver on their projects effectively
- Allow the HO managers who are heading overall projects, which are distributed across the HO and Offshore Centers, to achieve a higher success rate on their projects
- Allow the HO managers to be better rewarded for their efforts in offloading projects to Offshore Centers and ensuring their success, by better aligning their *key result areas* (KRAs) with the company's objective of saving costs by increased offshoring
- Offer new and additional offshoring-related roles and responsibilities to HO managers, to make their roles more critical for the company and to significantly enhance their contributions
- Allow the Offshore Center managers to significantly improve the productivity of their teams by increasing investments in employee hiring, training, and skill building without being severely constrained because of the company's excessive cost-saving expectations from the Offshore Center
- Allow the Offshore Center managers to get fair representation in company-wide global management committees, to win fair and just treatment for the Offshore Center employees on all matters
- Allow the Offshore Centers to make strategic contributions to their companies, instead of remaining just low-cost implementation centers
- Allow expatriate managers from the HO to the Offshore Centers to develop the requisite knowledge and skills to succeed in meeting the expectations of Offshore Center teams from their expatriate assignments
- Allow the company's executive management to decide the right role and responsibilities for their Offshore Center head, based on the company's characteristics and offshoring requirements
- Allow the Offshore Center head to get the requisite authority and control over the Offshore Center team, to lead and manage them effectively to make the Center deliver to its full potential

The Offshore Centers can then *rise to the next level* and make much more significant contributions to the revenues, cost savings/profits, and growth of their companies. The Offshore Centers can then play a major strategic and critical role for their companies, like the role being played by the HO, rather than being just low-cost implementation centers.

In the coming chapters, the book suggests techniques for the Offshore Center and HO managers to deal with the following challenges faced by Offshore Centers.

1. Global companies have long been outsourcing projects to services companies (vendors) that are not part of the company. Unfortunately, even when the HO management of a company offloads projects to its own Offshore Center, it treats the Offshore Center in a similar fashion as it treats the outsourcing vendors executing projects for it. The HO managers consider the Offshore Center as subordinate to the HO and expect the teams in the Center to simply follow instructions from the HO.

   This book shows that Offshore Center teams have a number of unique strengths that teams of outsourcing vendors lack. The book argues that HO managers will fail to capitalize on these strengths if they treat the Offshore Center in the same way as its outsourcing vendors. The book suggests that HO managers capitalize on these strengths by considering their Offshore Center teams as being truly a part of, and an extension to, the HO teams. The company will then be able to derive enhanced results from its Offshore Center teams, resulting in higher success rates of its projects.

2. Even if HO managers consider the Offshore Center to be part of the HO for most purposes, it is still a stark reality that a large number of Offshore Center projects are generally mere extensions to HO projects. The overall authority over these projects resides with the HO managers. The HO managers assume that the offshore project modules may not succeed if they do not have tight control over them, and hence, exert their direct authority over the Offshore Center project teams. The Offshore Center managers then end up handling huge project responsibilities without the requisite authority and freedom, which significantly constrains their ability to hire, retain, lead, motivate, and manage talent to deliver effectively on their project deliverables.

   This book suggests techniques that will give sufficient independence and decision-making authority to the Offshore Center managers to allow them to extract the best results from their teams. Thus, the quality and timeliness of project deliverables, and the productivity and morale of the Offshore Center teams, will improve considerably.

However, it should be noted that giving more authority and responsibilities to Offshore Center managers may possibly dilute the authority and responsibilities of the HO managers. This book addresses these concerns of HO managers by proposing new additional offshoring-related roles and responsibilities for these managers. The HO managers will then be playing a more critical role for the company, and will make much more significant contributions to the company compared to their current role. Further, the book suggests techniques to better align the KRAs of the HO managers with the company's objective of saving costs by increased offshoring, to allow the HO managers to be better rewarded for their performance in offloading projects to the Offshore Center and ensuring their success.

3. The work culture, management practices, employee sensitivities, career growth expectations, and employee designations/roles in the country of the Offshore Center can be quite different from those in the country of the HO. HO managers sometimes do not appreciate these nuances, and in their efforts to integrate the Offshore Center with the HO, impose HO norms on the Offshore Center teams, leading to employee displeasure, demotivation, and loss of productivity.

   This book elaborates the benefits of retaining the local norms in the Offshore Center and suggests techniques that will allow the Offshore Center to integrate with the HO but still retain its local work culture. The techniques will help meet the expectations and aspirations of the Offshore Center employees, which will motivate them to perform to their full potential.

4. Offshore Centers have many senior and highly capable managers and technical personnel. These professionals deserve to reach top management and top technical positions in the overall global company hierarchy. If they are in these top positions, they can help the company choose the right strategies for future revenue growth, visualize new potentially highly successful products, etc. Unfortunately, these Offshore Center senior professionals often do not get opportunities to grow to global top positions because of the constraint of their not being based in the HO. Instead, comparatively less capable HO personnel rise to global top positions purely on the basis of their location. Thus, although more capable and deserving professionals exist in the company, leaders are unable to fully utilize their potential, resulting in loss in revenues and profits for the company.

   This book suggests techniques that will allow the growth of deserving senior and capable Offshore Center employees to key global top positions based purely on their merit, and not constrained by their location. The global top management and technical positions will then be filled only by the most capable and deserving professionals in the company, who can then make the right strategic decisions to significantly increase the revenues and profits of the company.

5. In many companies, the Offshore Center management is not sufficiently represented in the company's global management committees that make decisions on overall company policies, management practices, employee appraisal norms, employee benefits, distribution of projects among various locations, resolution of interlocation contention among employees, selection of employees for global top positions, etc. The decisions made by such committees are then not in the best interest of the Offshore Center and its employees. The Offshore Center then fails to win a large number of projects, which limits the Center's growth and contribution to the company's revenues and cost savings. Further, Offshore Center employees fail to win decisions in their interest from these committees, resulting in employee demoralization and loss of productivity. The Offshore Center teams are then unable to add value to the company up to their full potential.

   This book highlights the problems that can occur because of lack of Offshore Center representation in these company-wide committees. The book suggests the right composition of these committees, with fair representation of the Offshore Center management. The Offshore Center managers on these committees can then sell the strengths of their teams to convince the company to offload large projects to the Center. They can also effectively raise the requirements and concerns of the Offshore Center employees in these committees to win the right decisions for them, in terms of getting favorable employee policies, benefits, career growth norms, and fair resolution of interlocation employee contentions.

6. HO management generally assumes that Offshore Center teams are not capable enough to deliver on large and complex projects. The Offshore Center is then typically given basic and peripheral activities, such as executing simple projects; basic features and additions to core products; maintenance of existing projects; etc. The Offshore Center is then adding a large number of employees to the company but is not working on new core products/projects, which might add huge revenues to the company compared to the low-revenue-generating peripheral projects usually being executed in the Center.

   Further, since the Offshore Center does not offer opportunities to work on challenging projects, it is unable to hire, retain, and motivate talent, especially capable and experienced professionals. The Offshore Center teams then consist of inexperienced and mediocre professionals, who may fail to deliver even on the simple projects assigned to them.

This book debunks the myth that Offshore Centers are not capable of delivering on large and complex projects. The book suggests techniques by which the Offshore Center management can convince the company to offload to them high-revenue-generating core, complex, and large projects. Thus, the full potential of Offshore Center teams is realized, leading to the Center making much greater contributions to the company's revenues.

7. Offshore Centers are established to achieve cost savings for the company, by offshoring projects to low-cost Offshore Center locations in countries that have lower salary costs and lower operating costs compared to the HO. However, many companies over-insist on the cost-saving factor, leading to inefficiencies in project delivery from the Offshore Centers. The excess pressures to control costs result in multiple problems in the Offshore Center—for example, the inability to hire capable employees since their salary expectations cannot be met; cutting down the investment in training and skill development of employees; and severely limiting the resources required to deliver results to the full potential of the employees. Thus, the output of the Offshore Center is reduced, resulting in an overall loss of revenues and profits of the company.

   This book suggests techniques for balancing the Offshore Center cost-saving requirements with the need to increase investment in the Center, for it to build its capacity to deliver to its full potential. The techniques will result in much higher revenues and cost savings for the company in the long run, which will more than offset the additional cost incurred in the Offshore Center in capacity building.

8. Offshore Centers recognize the contributions of their high-performing employees by instituting local awards in the Center. The employee delivering the best performance among all the Offshore Center employees is publically recognized and awarded. The purpose of such awards is to motivate the employees to perform beyond their potential to achieve such recognition. However, since the employees compete only with their peer Offshore Center employees, the competition to win the awards may not be that hard for high-performing employees. Such a competition does not force the employees to significantly improve their performance to win the awards, and the overall improvement in the productivity of the Offshore Center employees remains low.

   Since a large number of projects within the Offshore Center are extensions to the core projects being executed in the HO, employees in both locations are working on similar projects. This book suggests that companies capitalize on this fact by instituting *global awards*, where Offshore Center employees compete with the HO employees to win the awards.

The HO will usually have a number of high performers who are working on core and complex projects of the company. Thus, Offshore Center employees now have to compete not only with a larger population of employees, they are now up against many high performers who are excelling on core projects. The Offshore Center employees then have to stretch themselves much beyond their potential to win the awards, leading to much higher improvement in overall productivity in the Offshore Center.

9. An interesting area of debate over the past many years has been on the role to be played by the Offshore Center head. At one extreme, we have companies that are fully capitalizing on the strengths of their Offshore Center heads by giving them complete responsibility, authority, and control over the Offshore Center teams and projects. At the other extreme, we have companies that are running their Offshore Centers without a local head, with all the Offshore Center teams reporting directly to HO management. Companies need to judiciously decide the role, authority, and responsibilities of the Offshore Center head position to be able to derive the best results from the Offshore Centers.

Since each company has its unique characteristics and offshoring requirements, this book suggests that companies define the role and responsibilities of the Offshore Center head based on multiple factors, including the type and size of the company, the size of the Offshore Center and its growth plans, the company's senior management's knowledge about running a company in the country of the Offshore Center, the nature of projects to be offshored, ranging from totally independent projects to plain extensions of HO projects, etc. The book then elaborates the complete set of functions to be performed by the Offshore Center head based on these factors. The Offshore Center head can then lead, motivate, and manage the Offshore Center team successfully to ensure the success of the projects/activities in the Center, and thus to significantly increase the Center's contributions to the company.

10. HO managers sometimes need to travel to the Offshore Center on short-term or long-term expatriate assignments to accomplish specific tasks. Some examples of expatriate assignments can be an HO project manager transferring knowledge about his or her HO project to an Offshore Center team for them to execute some modules of the project; an HO division head establishing the extension of his or her division in the Offshore Center; and an HO senior management person being posted as expatriate Offshore Center head until a local head is hired for the Center.

The HO management personnel selected for expatriate assignments sometimes wrongly assume that their skills, experience, and working methods being used in handling their current management roles in the

HO will suffice in handling their expatriate assignments. However, since the roles and responsibilities of an expatriate manager are different from the normal management responsibilities within the HO, these HO managers may then fail to meet the expectations of their expatriate roles.

This book describes the differences in these roles and elaborates the new knowledge and skills that HO managers need to gain to prepare to handle expatriate assignments. The book suggests techniques that will allow these expatriate managers to meet the expectations of Offshore Center teams and add significant value to them.

11. In a large number of companies, the role of Offshore Centers is limited mostly to handling engineering functions of executing projects. Although companies have been growing the team sizes in their Offshore Centers, the value-add of the Offshore Centers to companies has still been limited because of their limited role. Most of the strategic functions of companies are still being performed by the HO. The HO decides the products to be developed by the company (for product development companies), the business and technology domains in which the company will execute services projects (for services companies), and the strategic acquisitions to be made by the company. The Offshore Center traditionally does not have a role to play in these strategic functions.

If Offshore Centers are to increase their contribution to their companies' revenues significantly, they should go much beyond handling plain engineering functions. This book suggests techniques that will allow Offshore Centers to perform the above-described strategic functions of conceiving new products, entering new domains for winning services projects, and making strategic acquisitions for the company. The Offshore Centers will then be able to increase their companies' revenues and cost savings significantly, and create many more new avenues of career growth for the Offshore Center employees.

A Note on Terminology

This book uses the term *manager* as a generic term to denote managers at all levels of the management hierarchy: first-level managers, mid-level managers, senior managers, and the top managers of the company. In instances where I want to refer specifically to a particular management level, I use specific terms such as *project manager* for first-level managers; and terms such as *engineering director*, *Offshore Center head*, *vice president*, etc., for higher-level managers.

Similarly, the book uses the generic term *management* to represent management teams at any level of the management hierarchy, and uses specific terms such as *project management, senior management,* and *top management/executive management* to denote the specific hierarchy of the management team.

This book uses the term *project team* as a generic term to refer to team members (and project managers) belonging to all the functions involved in executing an engineering project. These team members may belong to a range of functions related to the project—development, testing, configuration management, documentation, etc. Other stakeholders/professionals associated with an engineering project will be referred to by terms specific to their functions, such as *program managers, product managers,* etc.

Chapter 2

Be "Truly Global" in Outlook and Character

Global companies have long been outsourcing projects to services companies, also referred to as outsourcing vendors. These vendors are companies based in offshore countries, which have low costs of project execution. The head office (HO) management of these global companies exercises total control over the projects outsourced to these vendors. They make all the project decisions and generally expect the vendor execution teams simply to follow their instructions.

These global companies then set up their own Offshore Centers. Unfortunately, even when the company HO management offloads projects to its *own* Offshore Center, it treats the Offshore Center in a similar fashion as it treats its outsourcing vendors. The HO management considers the Offshore Center as subordinate to the HO and expects the Offshore Center teams simply to follow their instructions. Such behavior by the HO management is not in the right spirit of running Offshore Centers, and demoralizes the Offshore Center teams. The offshore teams then cannot perform to their full potential.

This book suggests the need to make the HO management consider their Offshore Center as being truly a part of, and an extension to, the HO. A company that has a HO and an Offshore Center should be treated the same as a company that has two offices in its own country, such as a Silicon Valley company that may have two engineering centers, in San Jose and Santa Clara. The Offshore Center should be treated at par with the HO for all practical purposes, and there should not be any subordination or discrimination based on location. Such a global outlook and character will make the HO management treat the Offshore Center teams with as much respect as its local HO teams.

Some global companies, indeed, have matured from the stage of treating their Offshore Centers as subordinates to considering these centers as extensions of the HO. However, the HO management still considers the Offshore Center teams to be weak and not as capable as the HO teams. Because of such an outlook, the HO management does not offload core and complex projects to the Offshore Center, does not involve the Offshore Center teams in the company's strategic activities, does not offer a similar global career growth path to the Offshore Center professionals as it offers to their HO counterparts, etc. These factors make the Offshore Center teams unable to deliver to their full potential. This chapter analyzes the core reasons for the concerns of HO managers that prevent them from treating the Offshore Center teams at par with the HO teams.

The rest of the chapters of this book will present detailed techniques to address these concerns, to allow companies to capitalize on the true strengths of their Offshore Center teams and realize their full potential.

2.1. Offshore Centers Are Not the Same as Outsourcing Vendors

The HO management in a global company will typically execute the company's offshoring strategy by following the timeline below.

- Start the process by offshoring small projects to outsourcing vendors in countries that provide cost savings during project execution.
- Gain confidence in the success of outsourcing upon successful execution of these projects.
- Outsource larger projects with large teams to these vendors.
- Once they realize that they have regular projects available for a large enough team to justify the cost savings of having an Offshore Center, set up the Center in the country with best available talent for their projects. Offload their future projects to their own Offshore Center instead of to outsourcing vendors.

Hence, the company's HO managers have experience working with outsourcing vendors for years before their own Offshore Center is established. They are now well aware of the mechanisms to be used for managing projects outsourced to vendors.

The HO management of the global company (also referred to as the "client" company) likes to keep tight control over their projects outsourced to vendors to ensure the success of the projects. They make all the decisions related to these outsourced projects. The project execution teams within these outsourcing vendors are considered as subordinate to the client company on all project-related matters and are expected simply to follow the instructions of the client.

The global company then matures to reach the next step of setting up its own Offshore Center. However, although the company sets up the Offshore Center, the HO managers keep following the same outsourcing practices as before. The result is the HO managers treat their own Offshore Center the same as an outsourcing vendor. The HO managers offload projects to the Offshore Center, make all the project-related decisions with a minimal say of the Offshore Center management/teams, exercise total control over the Offshore Center project teams, and expect these offshore teams simply to follow their instructions on all the project-related matters.

However, the HO managers should realize that there are some fundamental differences in outsourcing projects to vendors and offloading projects to their own Offshore Center. Since the Offshore Center is part of their own company, the Offshore Center teams have a number of unique strengths that may not be present in the outsourcing vendor teams. If the HO managers follow similar mechanisms in managing and controlling projects in both cases, they will fail to capitalize on these strengths of their Offshore Center teams.

Some of the unique strengths of Offshore Center teams, compared to outsourcing vendor teams, are described below.

1. HO managers have no role in hiring and training the team of the outsourcing vendor working on their projects. The outsourcing vendor selects a team that it believes has the best capability to execute the project.

   In contrast, the Offshore Center is an integral part of the company, and its management team works closely with the HO management team. HO management shares detailed information about the company's planned projects with the Offshore Center management. The Offshore Center management can then hire candidates with expertise and experience in the business/technical domains of these projects. These hired employees are then trained further on these domains of expertise.

   Thus, the teams in the Offshore Center have much deeper expertise and training in executing the offshored projects compared to the teams of outsourcing vendors.

2. Upon completion of an outsourced project, the outsourcing vendor may move the execution team members to a different outsourced project from a different client. These team members are then not available to execute the next version of the same project being outsourced by the current client company. These team members will have gained extensive expertise and experience in the domain of the project while executing it. Unfortunately, this expertise is no longer available for the future projects

in the same domain, since these team members have been moved to a project of another client. Thus, future projects being outsourced by the HO management suffer based on lack of domain experts required to execute the projects.

In contrast, the Offshore Center team members working on a project are earmarked as "domain experts" in the domain of the project. These team members are then assigned to work on the next versions of the same project, or on other projects in a similar business/technical domain. Over a period of time, these professionals will work on multiple projects in the same domain. Thus, the Offshore Center is able to develop a set of domain experts who are at par with their HO counterparts in terms of their knowledge, expertise, and experience in the company's business/technical domain of its core projects. Future similar projects offloaded to the Offshore Center will likely be highly successful, since these projects will utilize the services of these domain experts.

3. HO managers will want to protect the confidentiality and intellectual property rights (IPR) of the company and its projects, to keep ahead of the competition. Since the outsourcing vendor is a separate company, such information is normally not revealed to their teams. Thus, the HO managers reveal limited information on projects to the vendor teams, which justifies the reasons for all the project decisions and control residing with the HO management.

In contrast, the employees in the Offshore Center belong to the company itself, which allows them access to all the confidential information and IPRs related to the projects being executed by them. They have detailed insight into their projects, which allows them to participate in activities beyond plain execution of the projects. They have complete knowledge to make key project decisions and perform key project tasks independently, from project conceptualization to implementation.

Thus, Offshore Centers have strong teams with extensive skills, expertise, and experience for delivering on the projects of the company. If HO managers decide to exert total control over their projects and limit the Offshore Center team's role to plain execution of the HO's instructions on the project, that amounts to gross underutilization of the potential of the Offshore Center team. The Offshore Center team will feel suffocated and unmotivated if they are being prevented from taking control of their projects and are not allowed to perform to their full potential.

Further, the Offshore Center team also has deep understanding of the project IPR, which allows the team members to introduce innovations and optimizations in the project and help the company remain ahead of the competition.

If HO managers limit the role of the Offshore Center team only to plain project execution, that will eliminate innovation and optimization opportunities.

Instead, HO managers should capitalize on the strengths of the Offshore Center team by giving them independence and control over their projects. The Offshore Center team will then be able to perform effectively the key tasks of project conceptualization, innovation, architecture, design, implementation, and optimization. The managers will be able to derive better results from the Offshore Center team, resulting in higher revenues and cost savings for the company.

2.2. Offshore Center Teams Are Not Treated at Par with the Head Office Teams

A number of global companies have matured to a stage where they consider their Offshore Centers as a part of the global company and as extensions to their HO, instead of treating the Offshore Centers as outsourcing vendors. The HO managers in these companies have taken multiple steps to integrate the Offshore Centers with the HO, in terms of implementing similar engineering processes and project delivery mechanisms in the Offshore Centers as are applicable in the HO, where these HO managers are based.

Although the HO managers consider the Offshore Center as an integral part of the company, they still do not treat the Offshore Center teams at par with their local HO teams. They consider the Offshore Center teams to be less capable than the HO teams. Such an outlook by the HO managers creates a number of constraints for the Offshore Center teams.

- The company's core projects are still being executed in the HO, while the Offshore Center is being offloaded only extensions to these projects, or is given some other low-value simple and peripheral projects of the company. Thus, even though the company leaders have grown their Offshore Center team to a large size, the overall business value and contributions to the company's revenues from them is still limited.
- The role of the Offshore Center has been limited to just engineering functions of plain execution of projects. Let us consider the example of global product development companies. The HO managers are still not offloading strategic activities to the Offshore Center—for example, having input into deciding the company's core business strategies and new business/technology domains in which to develop future products along with interfacing with core customers to conceptualize new products.
- Offshore Center employees are not being offered similar growth opportunities in the global company hierarchy as their HO counterparts.

2.3. Concerns of Head Office Management

The above challenges and constraints faced by Offshore Center teams are not due to any deliberate design by HO management. Instead, these challenges are due to misgivings and concerns about the capabilities of the Offshore Center teams.

The HO management team makes many assumptions about the Offshore Center teams.

1. HO management believes that, because of the large salary difference between the country of the HO and the country of the Offshore Center, capable professionals from the country of the Offshore Center will have already relocated to make their careers in the country of the HO (or to some other country with similar high economic status). Hence, HO management assumes that the professionals joining their Offshore Center have only mediocre capabilities. This assumption makes the HO management think the Offshore Center teams cannot execute core and complex projects/activities. Thus, the Offshore Center is offloaded only simple, peripheral, and unchallenging tasks.

2. The key customers of the company reside mostly in the HO's country. The company's products need to cater to these customers. Hence, the product strategy, product management, product specifications, and architecture needs to be controlled from the HO, since it is not reasonable to offload these functions to a distant offshore country where the team has little visibility to its key customers.

   Hence, by default, all strategic functions and the core product development functions remain within the HO. The Offshore Center can then be offloaded only the engineering tasks of execution of some project modules, with the overall project control still residing with the HO management.

3. A corollary to the Offshore Center not handling core and strategic activities is that the managers and architects within the Offshore Center do not gain expertise and experience in handling complex tasks. Hence, they cannot be promoted to top management/technology roles within the overall company hierarchy because of fears of the company's global top management that they will not be able to deliver. The Offshore Center senior executives then cannot grow to assume the company's key global roles, and only their HO counterparts receive these roles.

This book suggests that Offshore Center management should recognize the above misgivings of HO management and then determine ways to address them to create a positive impression about the capabilities of the Offshore Center. The rest of the chapters of the book will describe multiple techniques that will allow the Offshore Center management to address these challenges and change the perception of the HO management about the Offshore Center teams' capabilities.

The HO management will then start assigning core and complex projects to the Offshore Centers, giving authority and control over these projects to the Offshore Center management, assigning core strategic activities to the Offshore Centers beyond plain project execution tasks, and offering growth opportunities to deserving Offshore Center professionals to key global top positions of the company. Thus, companies will be able to realize the full potential of their Offshore Center teams.

* * * * *

In Section 2.1 it was suggested that HO managers should capitalize on the strengths of the Offshore Center team by giving it independence and control over its projects. It should, however, be noted that many projects in the Offshore Center are extensions to HO projects. These projects will have some overlapping areas for which the overall control and decision-making authority will reside with HO management. Chapter 3 will discuss how to manage such distributed projects, by effectively balancing the authority and responsibility of the HO management and the Offshore Center management leading various modules of these projects.

Chapter 3

Authority and Freedom to Offshore Center Management

A large number of projects in the Offshore Center are extensions to head office (HO) projects. The overall projects are divided into modules, which are distributed among the HO and the Offshore Center. The overall authority of these projects resides with the HO managers.

When these distributed projects involve small teams, the HO managers can manage the Offshore Center project teams directly. However, as the team sizes increase, it becomes difficult for HO managers to control the Offshore Center teams directly, along with their HO teams. Thus, the control of the Offshore Center teams on these projects is then given to the management team within the Center, while the overall authority of the projects still resides with the HO managers.

HO managers assume that the modules of their projects being executed in the Offshore Center may not succeed if they do not have tight control over them. Thus, although the Offshore Center managers are responsible for delivering on these project modules and the offshore teams report directly to them, HO managers start exercising direct authority over these offshore teams. The management team in the Offshore Center is not given sufficient authority to make decisions independently for their teams and project modules.

Further, because of the cost-saving benefits of offshoring, companies grow the size of Offshore Center teams on such interlocation projects much larger than the size of the HO teams. For a typical project, a small number of project modules is executed in the HO by a small team, while a large number of project modules is executed in the Offshore Center by a significantly bigger team.

The HO managers responsible for the overall projects then end up managing very small teams in the HO directly, as compared to remotely located large Offshore Center teams on these projects. These HO managers feel that their authority and span of direct control over the teams has been significantly reduced. They start feeling insecure about slowly losing the complete projects and all their authority to the Offshore Center management. Such insecurities further push the HO managers to start controlling the Offshore Center teams directly, to demonstrate to the company senior management that they are still managing and controlling a large, interlocation team.

The Offshore Center managers have deep understanding of the strengths, aspirations, and job expectations of their local teams. Hence, they are best equipped to lead, motivate, and manage these teams to deliver on their project modules successfully. However, since these managers now lack authority and control over their teams, they are unable to manage their teams successfully.

The HO managers start exercising direct authority over the Offshore Center teams and start making project decisions for them, but because these managers are based in the HO, they have limited knowledge of the strengths of these remotely located teams compared to the knowledge of the Offshore Center managers to whom these teams directly report. Because of this limited knowledge, the HO managers start making incorrect decisions for the Offshore Center teams and their project modules. The Offshore Center project deliverables then tend to suffer from these decisions, which results in a negative impact on the overall project deliverables.

Further, the act of the HO managers in controlling the Offshore Center teams directly creates demoralization in the Offshore Center managers. The productivity of these managers and their teams is negatively impacted, leading to reduced output from the Offshore Center.

This chapter discerns the core reasons for such constraints being imposed on Offshore Center managers and teams. It suggests techniques that address these problems of the insecurities of the HO managers and the lack of authority and freedom with the Offshore Center managers. The suggested techniques facilitate mechanisms that offer additional roles and responsibilities to HO managers that can prevent dilution of their authority and direct span of control. The HO managers will then refrain from exerting direct control over the Offshore Center teams. They will, instead, give sufficient freedom and decision-making authority to the Offshore Center managers for them to extract the best results from their teams. The morale, motivation, and productivity of the Offshore Center managers and teams will then improve, leading to highly successful project deliveries.

3.1. Offshore Center Projects Are Extensions to Head Office Projects

It should be noted that offloading totally independent projects to the Offshore Center with complete delivery responsibility works best. Such mechanisms avoid the need to have complex interlocation management reporting structures and any associated problems. However, this situation is an ideal and is mostly infeasible in companies with Offshore Centers. The basic nature of offshoring results in a large number of Offshore Center projects being extensions to HO projects and being controlled from within the HO.

Let us consider the case of a product development global company running an Offshore Center. The company develops products for global customers, with specific focus on its key customers who generate the most revenues. When such a global company was first incorporated, the top management would obviously have chosen the location for the HO to be close to its potential key customers. Thus, the key customers of this global company would be based within the country of its HO.

Based on the requirements of these key customers, the company decides on new products to be developed and the major features to add to its existing products. These new products and features are planned by the product management teams in the company. The product management teams need to interact closely with these key customers to understand their pain points and new requirements, to decide the key product features. They need to work closely with these key customers to release product prototypes and initial nonproduction releases to them for their feedback and inputs. The product features are then refined and improved. The complete product is then developed, and the final "general release" of the product is delivered to all the company's customers around the globe.

Thus, the product management teams need to work closely with these key customers throughout the product release cycle. These teams should be based in proximity to these key customers for delivering successful products.

For all the above reasons, the product management teams are based in the HO of the company, which is based in the country of these key customers. Their presence in the HO results in products being conceived and planned from the HO. The overall product development is then controlled from within the HO.

The senior engineering management team and architects within the HO work closely with the product management team and decide the overall product specifications, architecture, and design. The core project modules for development of the product are assigned to the HO technical teams. The rest of the project modules are offloaded to the Offshore Center for development, while overall project execution control remains with HO management.

3.2. Overall Project Control Resides with the Head Office Management

The overall responsibility for implementation of this project for developing the product is assigned to a "project head" in the HO. The person is typically a senior management person designated as an "engineering director" or an "engineering senior director."

The project head then distributes modules of the project to the HO and Offshore Center technical teams. He or she prefers to keep core modules of the project in his or her location (the HO), for more effective project control, and assigns them to his subordinate project managers and their technical teams in the HO.

These HO project modules are the key modules of the project that control the overall functionality of the project. Typically, these modules are small in size and can be implemented by a small set of core professionals.

The other modules of the project are extensions to these core modules. These extension modules are then offloaded to the Offshore Center project managers and their technical teams.

It should be noted that the fact that the core modules reside within the HO does not imply that the project implementation team within the HO is larger than the team within the Offshore Center. Since the cost-saving benefit of executing the project in the Offshore Center is much higher than for executing the project within the HO, because of lower salary costs in the Offshore Center, typically a larger number of project modules is offloaded to the Offshore Center. Thus, the size of the technical teams working on the project is much larger in the Offshore Center than in the HO. The HO has only a small team of key professionals implementing the core project modules.

These offshore teams are managed by their respective project managers within the Offshore Center. These project managers report to an engineering director–level person, whom this chapter will refer to as the *Offshore Center director* (see Figure 3.1).

Companies create interlocation management reporting structures such that this Offshore Center director reports to the overall project head in the HO, whom this chapter will refer to as the *HO senior director*. This HO senior director also has a small number of local project managers and their teams reporting to him or her in the HO.

The overall responsibility of all the product development engineering activities in the company is with the vice president for engineering in the HO. He or she handles the overall responsibility for all the global engineering teams, in both the HO and the Offshore Center. The HO senior director, heading the project, reports to him.

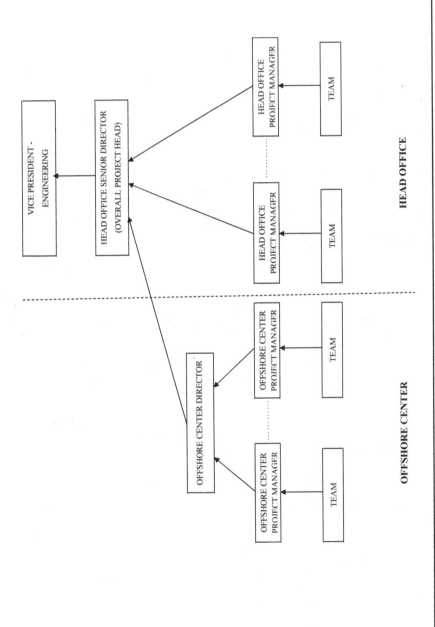

Figure 3-1 Interlocation management reporting structure.

3.3. Head Office Project Head Exercises Direct Authority over Offshore Center Teams

Unfortunately, some companies do not prescribe appropriate authority and responsibility division between the roles played by the Offshore Center management and the HO senior director, acting as the overall project head. Companies believe that since the overall project is being controlled from the HO, the HO senior director should be given enough authority and control over the offshore teams, if the project is to succeed. Company leaders then make the mistake of creating imbalance in authority of the HO and Offshore Center management, resulting in the authority over the Offshore Center teams being almost totally wielded with the HO senior director.

The Offshore Center director and project managers are responsible for leading and managing their teams to deliver the project modules assigned to them. However, the company does not give them sufficient authority over their teams for them to meet their project delivery responsibilities. The Offshore Center management is then unable to lead their teams effectively and may fail to deliver on their project modules.

Further, it has been observed that even if companies create the right authority and responsibility balance among the HO and Offshore Center management, the insecurities of the HO management can again cause the same problem of imbalance of authority. The HO senior director feels insecure about possibly losing his or her power because the majority of the project modules are offloaded to the Offshore Center to obtain cost savings. He or she realizes that he or she has a small size direct reporting team within the HO, while the Offshore Center director is leading a much larger team. The HO senior director feels that his or her authority and control span has been considerably weakened. He or she fears that in the future, he or she might lose the complete project to the Offshore Center.

The HO senior director realizes that, although, the Offshore Center director reports to him or her in the organization hierarchy, the Offshore Center director is still a direct competition and threat. He or she believes that the vice president could be aware that the Offshore Center director has all the qualifications and experience to take over the role of overall project head if needed.

The Offshore Center director is a senior professional with similar expertise, experience, and maturity level as the HO senior director. The Offshore Center director has been working for many years as a *second-level manager,* and hence has experience in managing first-level managers and their teams, a key requirement for handling the overall project head role. He or she also has extensive experience in handling strategic and operational management tasks required for the role.

Thus, the HO senior director has genuine fears that the company may decide to transfer the complete project to the Offshore Center and make the Offshore Center director the new overall project head, and he might lose his or her responsibility and job.

The HO senior director may then resort to tactics to demonstrate to the vice president, and higher management, that he or she is still handling the responsibility of a large team. He or she may start taking direct control of the project managers and their teams implementing their modules in the Offshore Center. He or she assigns them their tasks, instructs them during execution, monitors progress, etc. He or she may bypass the authority of the Offshore Center director and make all the important project decisions for the offshore teams. He or she may start managing the offshore teams in exactly the same way as he or she is managing his or her direct reporting project managers and their teams in the HO.

Thus, he or she tries to convince the vice president that he or she is managing the complete global team on the project, both his or her direct reporting HO teams and the Offshore Center teams. He or she tries to show that the results shown by the Offshore Center teams on their project modules are because of his or her leadership, and the role of the Offshore Center director is minimal.

3.4. Match Offshore Center Management Authority with Their Responsibilities

The actions of the HO senior director of directly controlling the offshore team create a number of problems for the Offshore Center director. The offshore team officially reports to the Offshore Center director for the project modules executed in the Offshore Center. He or she is responsible for leading and managing the team to ensure the success of the project. The company makes him or her *accountable* for the results of the project.

However, once the HO senior director starts directly controlling the Offshore Center team, the Offshore Center director ends up managing his or her team with virtually no authority. These constraints lead to a feeling of helplessness and frustration, demotivating him or her and the team, and severely impacts project deliverables.

It should be noted that the Offshore Center director is aware of the strengths and weaknesses of his or her team and is best equipped to make decisions for them in the best interest of their project modules. If the Offshore Center director is not allowed to make these decisions, or if his or her decisions are overruled, then the Offshore Center project modules will not be delivered on schedule and with high quality, which in turn will make the overall project fail to meet its objectives.

The Offshore Center director should highlight these facts to convince the vice president that he or she is much better equipped to lead and manage his or her local team than the HO senior director. He or she should ask the vice president to provide him or her authority to make all local decisions for his or her team by highlighting instances of problems in hiring, retaining, managing, and motivating team members if such authority resides in the HO management (see Case Study 3.1). He or she should justify his or her argument by sharing instances where projects succeeded because of his or her being able to lead and manage his or her team successfully by capitalizing on their strengths. He or she should also share instances where project deliverables suffered if the HO senior director controlled the activities of his or her team directly.

The vice president can thus be convinced to give the Offshore Center director complete authority and freedom over his or her team to deliver on the Offshore Center project modules and will prevent the HO senior director from controlling the team remotely.

3.5. Capitalize on Location Strengths

Once the vice president is convinced of the need to provide authority and control over the offshore project team to the Offshore Center director, he or she should then design authority and responsibility structures to implement the mechanisms.

The project modules within the Offshore Center are closely interlinked with the HO core project modules. Since the overall project control resides with the HO senior director, there could be a number of interlocation, project-related decisions that he or she oversees. There is a possibility that he or she could use these overlapping instances to exercise direct control over the offshore teams.

The vice president should clearly define policies and procedures to follow to prevent multiple potential interpretations of the authority and responsibilities in such overlapping scenarios. A simple rule to follow for this purpose is that the responsibilities and authority of respective managers should be according to their *location strengths*.

As discussed in the last section, the Offshore Center director is co-located with the offshore team, and hence he or she knows how to capitalize on their strengths to lead and manage them for their project modules. He or she should be given complete authority to make project decisions for the Offshore Center team to capitalize on this location strength.

The HO senior director is co-located with his or her HO team executing the core modules of the project. He or she understands the strengths of his or her team and knows how to lead, motivate, and manage them to deliver on the project objectives. Thus, he or she should be given full authority and control over this HO team executing the core modules of the project.

Further, the HO senior director has the advantage of being close to the product management team and major customers in the HO country. He or she should use these strengths to act as "project coordinator" for the Offshore Center team on the project and should perform the following tasks:

- Work closely with the product management team to develop an in-depth understanding of the complete product requirements.
- Work with the product management team to decide the scope of the current project release, in terms of selecting the subset of high-priority features to be implemented based on the available time and resources for the release.
- Divide the project work into modules.
- Work with the Offshore Center director to decide the set of modules to be offloaded to the Offshore Center.
- Offload the project modules to the Offshore Center.
- Decide intermediate project milestones and monitor progress of the Offshore Center project modules at these milestones.
- Interface regularly with the product management team to gather any ongoing project requirement changes information and share it with the Offshore Center director.
- Manage integration of Offshore Center project modules with the HO project modules.
- Ensure that the final project is released as per the project specifications.

The above mechanisms will ensure that the HO senior director role with respect to the Offshore Center project modules is limited to work distribution, information sharing, project monitoring, and integration tasks. The complete responsibility and authority for the Offshore Center project modules will reside with the Offshore Center director, since he or she can utilize his or her location strengths to deliver these modules successfully.

3.6. Head Office Project Head's Key Result Areas Not Aligned to the Company's Offshoring Objectives

The above mechanisms of clearly defining the authority and responsibilities of the Offshore Center director will give him or her the requisite authority to deliver on his or her project. The mechanisms will also prevent the HO senior director from impinging on the authority of the Offshore Center director over the offshore team.

However, it should be noted that these mechanisms still address only the *effect* of the core problem and do not address the *root cause* of the problem. The problem arose because the company decided to increase the size of the Offshore Center team for a project being controlled by the HO senior director. The HO senior director realized that his or her local HO team size is becoming small compared to the offshore team under the Offshore Center director. He or she started feeling insecure that slowly his or her complete project will be transferred to the Offshore Center and he or she may lose his or her responsibilities and job. Thus, he or she started controlling and managing the Offshore Center team directly, to show the vice president that he or she is still managing a large and multilocation team.

Once the vice president has implemented the mechanisms described in the last section, the HO senior director will no longer be able to control the offshore team directly. It will now become obvious to the vice president that the HO senior director is indeed managing *only* a small local team in the HO. The HO senior director will now feel even more insecure than before.

The insecurities of the HO senior director will make him or her resent the success of the Offshore Center director on his or her project modules. The HO senior director will be concerned that the success of project modules in the Offshore Center will lead to even further increases in the size of the offshore team, while reducing his or her span of control even more.

This resentment between the HO senior director and the Offshore Center director will not auger well for the overall project. The project modules in the HO and the Offshore Center are closely interlinked. The Offshore Center project modules are extensions to the HO core project modules. Thus, the Offshore Center director is heavily dependent on the HO senior director and needs his or her continuous support to ensure successful delivery of the Offshore Center project modules.

Further, the HO senior director is also the interface of the Offshore Center director to internal and external customers of the project—the product management team in the HO and the major customers in the HO's country. The Offshore Center director needs regular inputs and feedback from these customers to ensure the success of his or her project modules.

If the Offshore Center director faces resentment or noncooperation from the HO senior director, then he or she will fail to get crucial inputs and support on all the above critical aspects. Since the Offshore Center project modules cannot be implemented successfully without these critical inputs, there will be negative impacts on delivery of these modules. The Offshore Center director may then fail to deliver his or her project modules successfully.

The offshore project modules constitute a major part of the overall project. Any failure of these modules will result in the overall project also failing. Thus, the vice president needs to devise a comprehensive solution to address the root cause of the problem of insecurities of the HO senior director to ensure the success of the overall project.

The core reasons for the insecurities of the HO senior director can be traced to the mismatch of his or her key result areas (KRAs) and the company's offshoring objectives. The differences between his or her KRAs and the vice president's KRAs (which are aligned to the company's objectives) will be discussed next, and a method to align the two will be suggested to ensure the success of interlocation projects.

The vice president for engineering is responsible for leading engineering projects of the company, which are distributed across the HO and the Offshore Center. His or her one KRA is delivering these projects on schedule and with high quality.

He or she also has the responsibility of controlling the costs of executing these projects, to increase the profit margins of the company. Offshore Centers provide a cost advantage for executing projects compared to executing projects in the HO. The vice president reduces the project costs by increasing the size of the Offshore Center teams and offloading larger chunks of the projects to them. Thus, his or her KRA matches the company offshoring objectives.

The company evaluates the performance of the vice president based on the results shown on these KRAs. If he or she has been able to increase the size of the offshore teams significantly, then he or she will have demonstrated a reduction in costs of the projects being executed, compared to executing major portions of the projects in the HO. He or she gets better performance ratings, salary increases, bonuses, and other monetary rewards if he or she increases the Offshore Center team size to much larger than the HO team size. Thus, he or she is highly incentivized to increase the Offshore Center team size and works wholeheartedly to meet this objective.

In contrast, in a number of companies, the HO senior director has a different set of KRAs, with no incentives to increase the Offshore Center team size. His or her KRA is to manage his or her team to deliver his or her project within schedule and with high quality. His or her performance rating and monetary rewards are linked to his or her success on delivering on this KRA.

Thus, he or she works toward making his or her project successful. It should be noted, however, that he or she is heading the *overall* project, which is distributed across the HO and the Offshore Center. He or she is rewarded not only for the success of project modules being executed by his or her direct reporting team in the HO, but also for the success of the project modules being executed in the Offshore Center. The success of the Offshore Center project modules of the overall project also contributes to his or her performance ratings and monetary rewards.

Since the HO senior director is incentivized to ensure the success of the project modules within the Offshore Center, one might assume that this will motivate him or her to strengthen the Offshore Center teams, increase their size, and offload more project modules to them. However, the catch here is that although the HO senior director is incentivized for the success of the overall project (including the Offshore Center project modules), he or she is *not* incentivized to increase offshoring to reduce the overall cost of executing the project.

A major reason why an Offshore Center team size is increased, compared to the HO team size, is the cost savings of executing the project in a low-cost offshore location. Since the HO senior director has no incentive to reduce the cost by increased offshoring, he or she will prefer to grow the HO team size and execute the majority of the project modules within the HO. He or she can decide to keep the Offshore Center team size on his or her project to a bare minimum, just to maintain a semblance that he or she is offshoring parts of his or her project.

The HO senior director believes that such a strategy will give him or her multiple benefits:

1. Since most of the team is close to him or her in the HO, he or she can manage and control their project work directly. He or she may believe that such close monitoring will give him or her better results than spending time and effort on remotely managing a large team in the Offshore Center. Further, since the Offshore Center will be delivering fewer project modules, the HO senior director may believe that it will take less time and effort to integrate them with the HO core project modules, compared to the scenario where a large number of offshore modules need to be integrated. Thus, considering all these perceived benefits, he or she would prefer to grow his or her HO project team rather than the Offshore Center team.

2. The HO senior director will then be directly managing a large team in HO. He or she can demonstrate to the vice president that he or she is indeed handling a large responsibility. Since the Offshore Center director will be managing only a small part of the overall project team, the vice president will not think of promoting him or her to an overall project head role, which would be a possibility if the Offshore Center director was managing the major part of the overall project. Thus, all these factors will make the HO senior director safe and secure in his or her job, without fearing that he or she may lose his responsibilities and job to the Offshore Center director.

The company's objectives are to grow the Offshore Center team size to reduce the project costs. However, the HO senior director is working totally opposite to this objective, instead increasing the HO team size instead of the offshore team size. His or her objectives are not aligned to the company's objectives.

3.7. Additional Responsibilities of Head Office Management to Address Their Insecurities

The vice president must provide a comprehensive solution to address the concerns about job insecurity of the HO senior director, align his or her KRAs to the company's objectives of growing the offshore teams, and ensure cooperation between him or her and the Offshore Center director. This purpose can be achieved by the following means.

3.7.1. Additional Head Office Projects

The HO senior director was directly managing a large team in HO before offshoring led to his or her HO team size being reduced. He or she is feeling insecure based on the reduction in his or her direct span of control and dilution of his or her authority. The vice president should address these insecurities by assigning the HO senior director additional responsibilities within the HO, which will make him or her feel that his or her authority and responsibilities have remained at the same level as before, even after offshoring a large part of his or her project and reduction in his or her HO team size.

The vice president can assign the HO senior director responsibility for leading an additional project within the HO, along with his or her current project. He or she will then be managing multiple teams within the HO and will realize that his or her total direct reporting team size has not been significantly reduced.

3.7.2. Project Coordinator for Independent Offshore Center Projects

Another option to increase the HO senior director's authority and span of control is to give him or her an additional responsibility that capitalizes on his or her strengths in managing interlocation projects. It was described in Section 3.5 that the HO senior director's major role in his or her current interlocation project is of being the "project coordinator" for the overall project. The section described the set of responsibilities he or she handles in this role—from working closely with the HO product management team in deciding project specifications and managing any changes in requirements to offloading (and finally integrating) appropriate project modules to the Offshore Center.

The vice president can decide to run some additional projects *totally independently* within the Offshore Center. The project team will reside totally in the Offshore Center under the Offshore Center director. The team will execute the complete project and deliver it to HO. No modules of this project will be executed within the HO.

Although the Offshore Center director of this independent project will have the management expertise and experience to deliver on it, it should be noted that the company's product management and key customers are still based in the HO. The HO senior director is based in the same location as the product management team. During the execution of his or her current interlocation project, he or she has learned techniques to work closely with the product management team and act as their interface with the Offshore Center director.

The vice president can then utilize this expertise of the HO senior director by assigning him or her the role of being a *partial* project coordinator for this additional completely offshored independent project. The HO senior director then becomes the interface for the Offshore Center director with the HO product management team and key customers for this independent project. He or she is assigned a subset of project coordinator responsibilities described in Section 3.5, in terms of performing the following tasks:

- Work closely with the product management team to develop deep understanding of the complete product features.
- Work with product management and the Offshore Center director to decide the scope of the current project release, in terms of selecting the subset of high-priority features to be implemented based on the available time and resources for the release.
- Share any ongoing project requirement changes information regularly to the Offshore Center director by interfacing with the product management team.
- Help and support the Offshore Center director in ensuring that the final project is delivered as per the project specifications.

Thus, again, the HO senior director will be reassured that since he or she is now handling an additional role, he or she is still handling critical responsibilities for the company. He or she was earlier managing only a single project. He or she will realize that his or her contributions are now more valuable than before, since he or she now has *critical roles* to play in *multiple projects*. He or she will not feel insecure about his or her job, despite his or her small direct reporting team size.

3.7.3. Align His or Her Key Result Areas to the Company's Offshoring Objectives

As discussed in Section 3.6, one KRA for the vice president is to control the cost of execution of the projects under him or her through offshoring, to increase the company's profit margins. He or she reduces the project costs by increasing the size of the Offshore Center teams and offloading larger chunks of the projects to them.

In contrast, in a number of companies, the HO senior director has no such KRA of increasing offshoring, and thus is not incentivized to grow Offshore Center team size to control project costs.

The vice president should align both of their KRAs by assigning this new KRA to the HO senior director to control the execution cost of his or her project through offshoring. If the HO senior director is able to significantly increase the size of the Offshore Center team working on his or her interlocation project, then the overall cost of the project will be reduced by a large margin. He or she will then be given high performance ratings and monetary rewards at the time of his or her performance appraisal.

The HO senior director is then be incentivized to increase the offshoring component and offshore team size for his or her project. He or she will work toward meeting these objectives, which align to the company's overall objectives of reducing costs by increasing the Offshore Center's size.

He or she will then not resent the Offshore Center director and the growth of offshore team size, but will help and aid the Offshore Center director in the process. The two of them will cooperate closely in ensuring success of their interlocation project and controlling its execution cost.

Each time the vice president plans to expand the offshore team size for the overall project being managed by the HO senior director, he or she should take the HO senior director into his or her confidence, consult him or her, and take his or her inputs in making the expansion decision.

The HO senior director has extensive experience in managing his or her project and similar past projects in the HO. He or she will tap into this vast experience to give highly valuable inputs to the vice president on the right strategy to be adopted for expanding the offshore team size. He or she will give inputs on:

- Necessary increase in the Offshore Center's team size for the project
- Project modules to be offloaded to this expanded offshore team, based on the skills and competencies required for executing these project modules and the strengths of the Offshore Center team
- Skills and experience required for any new professionals to be hired

- Internal and external training to be imparted to these Offshore Center professionals for them to deliver on their project modules, etc.

The vice president will then be able to make correct decisions about increasing Offshore Center teams, and these interlocation projects will be delivered successfully.

Case Study 3.1

A global leading product development company had a senior director in the HO managing a multilocation project for developing a new product. A large part of the project team was based in the Offshore Center and a small part of the team was in the HO. The Offshore Center component of the project consisted of multiple modules, with each module being managed by a project manager in the Center. These Offshore Center project managers reported directly to the HO senior director.

As the project grew in size, the vice president for engineering realized that the HO senior director was not able to manage the large multilocation team. He hired an engineering director in the Offshore Center to manage the Offshore Center team of the project, and all the local project managers reported to him. The Offshore Center project team size was then significantly increased, with the addition of more project managers and team members.

Since the HO senior director was now handling a small direct reporting team, he felt that his authority had been significantly eroded. He started feeling insecure about his job, suspecting that slowly the complete project would be transferred to the Offshore Center, and his role would be taken over by the Offshore Center director. He started resorting to tactics to exercise direct control over the Offshore Center team, to demonstrate to the vice president that he was still handling a major responsibility.

He started interviewing new candidates for Offshore Center hiring, started instructing the Offshore Center project managers/team members, ignored the Offshore Center director on multiple instances, etc.

Such actions severely impacted the Offshore Center delivery capability. For example, the HO senior director insisted that after the Offshore Center director and his team interviewed and decided to hire candidates, the candidates must be then interviewed by the HO senior director's subordinate project managers in the HO, followed by his final approval. Thus, all the hiring decisions needed to wait for a long time to be approved by appropriate authorities within the HO.

Excellent candidates generally have multiple job offers in hand. These candidates need to know the company's hiring decision quickly so they can make their career choice among these job offers. These candidates' interviews with the HO senior director and project managers needed to be scheduled from the HO, and multiple interviews needed to be conducted. Given the difference of almost half a day between the time zones of the Offshore Center and the HO, these tasks consumed many days to complete. Further, the salary decision for a selected candidate also took days to be closed, pending multiple approvals from the HO senior director and various other personnel within the HO.

These candidates would by then have joined another company, which made its decisions faster because hiring authority resided with their local heads. Hence, the Offshore Center lost the opportunity to hire excellent candidates.

Meanwhile, some major developments were taking place on the business front. The product management team realized that their core competition was going to release a similar product before their own project release date. It was decided to advance the release date of the project by prioritizing the features and including the most important features in the current release, and postponing the rest of the features to the next release.

The Offshore Center director was responsible for delivering the Offshore Center component of the project within this new curtailed time frame. He had been working closely with the product management team throughout the project execution and had developed a deep knowledge about the complexity of the product features and the expertise, time, and effort required to deliver them.

He stopped the ongoing work on low-priority features in the project and freed the team members working on them to support higher-priority ones. Since he had been working closely with his teams, he had gained deep under-standing of their expertise and strengths. Based on this knowledge, he transferred these freed engineers from their current teams to the teams working on high-priority features that fell within their domain of expertise and strength. Thus, the teams working on high-priority features were now strengthened with additional team members who had the expertise to deliver these features within the new tight schedules.

Besides shuffling engineers between various teams, Offshore Center director also realized that some other drastic measures would need to be adopted if the new project deadline was to be met. He analyzed the complexity of a couple of highest-priority features and estimated the time and effort required to imple-ment them. These features were originally assigned to a team under one of his subordinate project managers. He knew the strengths of the project manager and realized the manager had the expertise and strength to deliver these features as per the earlier schedule but would not be able to meet the new tight schedule. He analyzed the strengths and workload of his other subordinate project man-agers and made the judgment that one of them would be able to meet the new deadline for these features. He assigned the responsibility for delivering these features to this manager. He transferred the *complete technical team* working on these features from the current manager to this identified manager, while letting the current manager handle some other features. Thus, he was now confident that the highest-priority features would be delivered within the new tight delivery schedules.

Meanwhile, the HO senior director started exerting more control over the Offshore Center teams. He argued that since he was responsible for the *overall project,* he was concerned that it would be difficult for the Offshore Center teams to meet the challenges of delivering under the new tight schedules unless he was personally leading and guiding these offshore teams. He further argued that since he was closer to the HO product management team, he had a better understanding of the complexity of various features compared to the remotely located Offshore Center director. He would be able to capitalize on his knowledge of product features to make the right decisions for the Offshore Center teams implementing these features.

The HO senior director started taking direct control of the Offshore Center project managers and their teams working on some of the features. He started instructing these teams directly, bypassing the Offshore Center director in the process. He made decisions on the reassignment of team members to the high-priority features.

However, although he may have been more expert than the Offshore Center director in judging the complexity of the product features, he had limited knowledge of the strengths of the Offshore Center project managers and team members in delivering on these features. He had earlier managed the Offshore Center project team directly and knew the strengths of some of its team members, but at that time the team size was small. The Offshore Center project team had now significantly expanded, and many more team members and project managers had joined about whom he had only indirect knowledge, through the Offshore Center director. He could not match the right team member to be reassigned to the right feature and made some wrong reassignment decisions in the process.

Further, given his limited knowledge of the strengths of the Offshore Center project managers, he decided to play it safe and not take any drastic action of shuffling a complete feature (along with the team working on it) from one manager to another manager with better expertise and strengths to deliver on the feature under the new tight schedule. He did not realize that the current manager would have delivered the feature as per the original project schedule, but this manager lacked the skills to meet the challenge of delivering within the new tight schedule.

The Offshore Center director became totally frustrated by the HO senior director's actions. He started to face numerous problems in managing his Offshore Center team to deliver on the project:

1. He was unable to hire good candidates under the HO senior director's insistence on controlling the hiring process, which caused long delays in making job offers to candidates.
2. He realized that the HO senior director was assigning the incorrect set of team members and project managers to various high-priority features, and they would not be able to deliver as per the new tight schedule.
3. He was no longer in control of a large part of his team, and they were no longer following his decisions and instructions, since the HO senior director was overriding these instructions.

The Offshore Center director fully realized that he was now managing his team with virtually no authority and control. He could see that his project might fail because of the series of wrong decisions of the HO senior director, but he could do absolutely nothing to prevent that happening.

He was also aware that the HO senior director was virtually controlling his teams directly, but *officially* he was still in charge of the Offshore Center component of the project. If the project failed, he would be held accountable, and the HO senior director would take no responsibility for the failure. He became so frustrated with the situation that he *quit the company*.

The HO senior director was now officially directly responsible for the Offshore Center teams and project modules. However, because of his lack of knowledge of the strengths of the managers and team members, he kept making incorrect decisions about reassigning project features to team members. These personnel were unable to deliver successfully, and their project modules started slipping the intermediate milestones.

The HO senior director felt totally helpless in the situation, as he did not know how to bring the project back on track. He started spending extensive amounts of time and energy with the Offshore Center managers and teams in an attempt to make them succeed.

Thus, the amount of time he could now spend on interacting with his own HO team was reduced significantly. His own HO team therefore also started slipping on the delivery of the core modules of the project.

Finally, the overall project missed its new release schedule considerably, with *both* the project components within the Offshore Center and within the HO failing to meet their schedules. The competition had already released its product and had started capturing the market. Thus, the company experienced a major revenue loss from this failure.

The HO senior director had taken direct control of the Offshore Center team to show to the vice president that he also had strengths in managing the offshore team along with his HO team. The irony was that not only did he fail to deliver on the offshore project component, he was seen to be weak even in delivering on his own HO project component, which he used to deliver successfully in his earlier projects.

The vice president realized that it was not possible for the HO senior director to manage the Offshore Center team remotely, given the large team size. The situation was back to square one, with the vice president starting to look out to hire a new Offshore Center director for the project.

Solution

The Offshore Center director should have shared with the vice president some instances of challenges he was facing in hiring good talent. He should have shared that since he lacked the interviewing and decision-making authority and it was being handled by the HO management, it was causing long delays in making hiring decisions. He should have shared profiles of some highly experienced and capable candidates who did not join the company because they received job offers from other companies much sooner.

The vice president would have then realized that the Offshore Center was unnecessarily losing some excellent candidates given the delays caused by actions of the HO senior director in controlling the hiring process. He would be worried that such happenings were weakening the Offshore Center and would like to evolve ways to avoid this problem.

The Offshore Center director should have then impressed on the vice president that the Offshore Center had experienced and capable managers and technical people with the strength to interview and judge the right candidates for the Offshore Center positions. He should have also informed the vice president that although he would like the decisions on hiring of candidates for *most of the positions* to be made by Offshore Center management itself, he was flexible in involving some HO personnel in the hiring process for some critical Offshore Center positions that required close interactions with the HO.

One example of an Offshore Center position for which HO would need to be involved in the hiring decision-making process might be the architect position for Offshore Center project component. The overall product architecture is designed by the core architect within the HO. The HO architect then offloads to the Offshore Center architect the work of designing the architecture for the offshore project modules, which can be looked at as *extensions* to the core product architecture. Since these architectures are closely interlinked, the Offshore Center architect needs to work closely with the HO architect. Thus, the HO architect must also evaluate a candidate being hired for the Offshore Center architect position to be sure he is technically strong enough to meet his requirements of extending the core product architecture to the architecture of the offshore project modules.

The Offshore Center director should have informed the vice president that he would ensure such critical candidates were also interviewed by the right HO personnel and would jointly make decisions on their hiring.

The vice president would have then been convinced that the Offshore Center management had the capability to interview and hire good candidates. He would also appreciate the fact that the Offshore Center director was experienced and mature enough to judge a set of positions for which to involve HO personnel in the hiring process, to ensure that only the most relevant candidates were hired. He would have then given the authority and freedom on hiring decisions for the Offshore Center to the Offshore Center director. The Offshore Center director would have then made decisions on whether or not to involve HO personnel in specific hiring decisions.

The Offshore Center director should have also shared with the vice president instances of challenges in managing his team effectively with the HO senior director trying to control the team remotely. He should have stressed that he was more knowledgeable about strengths, expectations, and aspirations of his local team, and hence, could lead them effectively to delivery as compared to their being remotely controlled from HO.

Since the HO senior director had started controlling some Offshore Center project modules, the negative effects were becoming visible. With his lack of knowledge of the strengths of the Offshore Center personnel, he had assigned some high-priority features to a manager and team members who did not have the requisite expertise and strengths. The team was unable to deliver effectively, and these modules started slipping their intermediate schedules.

The Offshore Center director should have shared these instances with the vice president. He should have also shared that, in contrast, his directly controlled team was delivering the high-priority features being executed by them on schedule, since he had assigned tasks to team members according to their strengths.

The vice president would have then realized that the Offshore Center director was the most knowledgeable about the strengths of the Offshore Center team and was best equipped to lead them to deliver the project on schedule. He would have also realized that the efforts of the HO senior director to control the team remotely were failing to deliver successful results and could result in project failure and loss of revenue to the company. He would have then given the Offshore Center director full control over his team and would have prevented the HO senior director from exercising direct control over the team.

The vice president should have had a detailed talk with the HO senior director to understand the core reasons why he was exercising direct control over the Offshore Center team. He would have then realized that the core reason was that the HO senior director was feeling insecure and felt he was losing his authority and span of control as major parts of his project were offshored.

The vice president could have then assigned an additional role to the HO senior director to address his insecurities. The HO senior director could have been given project management responsibility for an additional HO team working on a different project. The HO senior director would now be managing larger HO teams with multiple projects, and he would not feel insecure.

The HO senior director would have then been happy to limit his role to being the "project coordinator" for the Offshore Center project component of the current project. He would not have felt insecure about the success and growth of the Offshore Center team but would have instead helped the Offshore Center director in this respect.

The HO senior director and the Offshore Center director would have then utilized their *complementary* location strengths to ensure the success of the project under new tight schedules.

The HO senior director had the location advantage of being close to the product management, which gave him deep insight to the high-priority product features planned to be included in the current release. He would have then shared this insight about the complexity of these features to the Offshore Center director, for the latter to judge the expertise, time, and effort required to implement these features.

The Offshore Center director had the location advantage of knowing the expertise and strengths of his local Offshore Center team. He would have utilized this knowledge to reassign the high-priority features to the managers and team members with the right strengths to deliver these features.

Thus, close cooperation between them would have resulted in the high-priority features being delivered successfully within the new tight schedule of the current project release.

* * * * *

This chapter discussed that many projects being executed in the HO and the Offshore Center are closely interlinked. The HO management meets the objective of integrating these projects by applying the HO norms on the Offshore Center for project management aspects, such as having similar documentation standards and project delivery processes for execution of projects in both locations. However, in some companies, the HO management starts imposing the HO norms on the Offshore Center on aspects beyond project management, leading to Offshore Center employee resentment and displeasure. Chapter 4 will discuss that since the Offshore Center is in a different country than the HO, it must retain the unique work culture, management practices, employee sensitivities, employee career growth expectations, and other related norms of its country, despite being a part of a global setup. Techniques to achieve this objective will be discussed and their benefits will be presented.

Chapter 4

Integrate Offshore Center with Head Office but Retain Local Work Culture

The Offshore Center and the head office (HO) of the company are based in different countries. Each country has its own unique work culture, management practices, employee sensitivities, employee career growth expectations, and other related norms. The employees in the Offshore Center would like to keep following these norms of their local country despite being a part of a global setup.

The HO management, in its bid to integrate the Offshore Center with the HO, sometimes makes the mistake of imposing the norms being followed in the HO on the Offshore Center. Such actions of the HO management cause resentment and displeasure among the Offshore Center employees. The employees feel demotivated, and their productivity and results are negatively impacted.

This chapter discusses the reasons for which the HO management imposes the HO norms on the Offshore Center. It presents arguments against this flawed approach. The chapter then elaborates with examples of some aspects where the HO management needs to respect the work culture and sensitivities of the Offshore Center—necessary to retaining the employee career growth norms and designations, handling employee retrenchment with deep consideration of local sensitivities, and being sensitive to employees' work–life balance by making the HO and Offshore Center share the pain that is often due to the time-zone difference between the two locations. The chapter concludes by suggesting a solution to address these problems by creating a local management committee within the Offshore Center that refines the HO norms as per the local work culture and sensitivities before implementing them in the Offshore Center.

4.1. Avoid Imposing Head Office Norms on the Offshore Center

The HO management sometimes lacks sufficient knowledge about the work culture, management practices, processes, employee career growth aspirations, employee designations, and employee sensitivities of the country of the Offshore Center. Based on this ignorance, the HO management starts imposing the norms being followed within the HO on the Offshore Center.

In some other cases, the HO management may have some preconceived notions about the norms being followed within the country of the Offshore Center. They then make decisions for the Offshore Center as per those notions.

Unfortunately, in both these cases, the actions of the HO management have a significant negative impact on the Offshore Center teams, leading to lowering their morale and productivity. The following are some of the problems faced by the Offshore Center employees because of such actions.

1. The Offshore Center employees have been following the work culture and the management practices prevalent in their country for many years. They have evolved working mechanisms that allow them to deliver efficiently as per these practices.

   The HO management now imposes the HO practices on the Offshore Center. The Offshore Center employees face problems adopting these totally different practices from the ones they have been following. Their working mechanisms that used to deliver excellent results now fail to deliver under the framework of these HO practices.

   In fact, the problem is more intense for the senior and highly experienced professionals in the Offshore Center. They have been following their prevalent practices for *many long years* and find it much more difficult to adjust to these new HO practices, compared to junior professionals. They start failing on their project deliverables because of these problems.

   These senior professionals are the core members of the Offshore Center project teams. The project teams depend on the strengths of these core professionals for the success of their projects. When these core professionals start failing on their project assignments, the projects themselves fail.

   Although the HO management notices that projects are failing in the Offshore Center, it cannot judge the reasons for these failures. The HO management refuses to believe that these problems could be occurring because of their imposing HO practices on the Offshore Center. They think that these very practices have been used in the HO for many long years with highly successful project deliveries and hence cannot be faulted. Unfortunately, they fail to realize that they are now imposing these practices in a different country with a totally different work environment and prevalent practices.

Thus, imposition of HO practices on the Offshore Center, without regard to the Offshore Center ground realities, results in failed projects and significantly reduced output from the Offshore Center.

2. The employee career growth norms and designations can differ between the countries of the HO and the Offshore Center. The Offshore Center employees set their growth expectations as per their local country norms.

    The HO management sets similar growth norms in the Offshore Center as are applied in the HO. The performing Offshore Center professionals are then provided a career growth path as per the HO norms in terms of their promotions and designations. However, these HO norms may not match the more attractive career growth norms being followed in the companies within the country of the Offshore Center. The Offshore Center professionals do not compare their career growth and designations with their HO counterpart professionals; they compare them with their peers in local industry. They then come to believe that they are not getting the career growth they deserve, despite performing well. They feel demoralized and may even decide to quit the Offshore Center to join some local company in their country, who provide them more attractive career growth, roles, and designations.

    The HO management fails to realize the reasons for the displeasure of the Offshore Center employees. The HO management believes that they are offering excellent growth path to the Offshore Center employees, *as per the norms being followed in the HO,* and the Offshore Center employees should have no reasons to complain.

    Thus, imposition of HO career growth norms results in displeasure and demotivation among high-performing Offshore Center employees and can result in loss of productivity and even attrition.

3. Sensitivities of people vary a lot between different countries. Professionals in the country of the Offshore Center may be very sensitive to issues that may be considered normal in the country of the HO.

    Since the HO management and teams would not understand such nuances, they may take some actions or utter some words, *with absolutely no ill intent,* that can severely hurt the sensitivities of the Offshore Center employees. The Offshore Center employees then assume that the HO is deliberately being insensitive to them and lacks respect for their sensibilities. These Offshore Center employees are then emotionally traumatized and demoralized, which reflects in significant lowering of their performance levels. Highly sensitive employees may even decide to quit the company, rather than protest such insensitive actions of the HO.

The HO management will have been taking such actions for their HO employees for many long years and never received any negative feedback, since these actions are not considered insensitive in their own country. Thus, the HO management fails to realize the damage they are doing to the Offshore Center employees by their actions and may even end up repeating these actions over and over again.

4. Further, the word on all the above acts of the HO management spreads in the industry in the country of the Offshore Center. The professionals in the industry then start carrying a negative image of the way the company is treating its Offshore Center employees. They assume that the HO management of the company is arrogant, dominating, inflexible, insensitive, and lacks respect for the contributions of its Offshore Center employees. The Offshore Center now has problems recruiting new employees, since capable professionals in the industry are not interested in joining such a Center.

Thus, the acts of the HO management of imposing the HO norms on the Offshore Center result in the Offshore Center having problems in hiring, retaining, and motivating their employees. The Offshore Center teams fail to deliver to their potential, and their project deliverables suffer.

The next sections discuss some examples of the negative impact of some actions of the HO management in imposing the HO norms on the Offshore Center teams without considering the local work culture and sensitivities.

4.2. Retain Offshore Center Career Growth Norms and Designations

The employee career growth norms and designations may be quite different between the countries of the HO and the Offshore Center. For example, employees in the technical ladder in U.S. companies generally have designations that clearly reflect their role and experience, such as member technical staff (MTS), senior MTS (SMTS), etc. However, senior technical personnel with similar experience in India, for example, have much more attractive designations, such as being designated as a technical lead/project leader/assistant manager instead of being simply called a SMTS.

The projects in the HO and the Offshore Center are quite interlinked. The Offshore Center team members generally execute modules of the same overall project that their counterpart team members in the HO are executing. The HO management believes that since all these employees are working on the same project and have similar roles and responsibilities, they should all have similar designations that reflect their roles in the project. Thus, the HO management decides to designate the Offshore Center employees in a similar fashion as their HO counterparts.

If the HO designations are imposed on the Offshore Center, these designations may not seem attractive to the Offshore Center employees. For example, an Offshore Center employee will not like to be designated as a SMTS, while his or her peers with similar experience are designated as "assistant managers" in other companies in his or her country. He or she would feel slighted and think that his or her status and respect in the society is being lowered. He or she may even decide to quit the Offshore Center to join a company that offers him or her a fancy designation as per the norms prevalent in that country.

Hence, companies should decide the local designations of the employees of the Offshore Center as per the norms being followed in their country. Of course, HO management also wants to know the actual role being played by the Offshore Center employees in their overall projects, regardless of their fancy local designations. This requirement can be met by assigning "dual designations" to the Offshore Center employees. For example, an employee designated locally as an "assistant manager" in the Offshore Center would be considered as a SMTS in the overall company hierarchy.

Similar dual designations should be used for the management team members of the Offshore Center. For example, the Offshore Center head might be designated locally as the CEO of the Center, while he or she would be designated as a "vice president" in the overall global company hierarchy.

Case Study 4.1

A U.S.-based software company was running an Offshore Center in India. Employee growth aspirations differ between these two countries. In the United States, a large number of software professionals want to specialize in their technical domains and remain in technical roles their entire career. In India, on the other hand, a number of professionals look for all-round growth and want to handle both technical and managerial responsibilities during their careers. Thus, a number of personnel in the technical ladder switch to management roles, such as, for example, after eight years of experience. With this difference in career growth aspirations of professionals in these countries, a number of professionals in the technical ladder in India may be younger and have less experience than such professionals in United States.

Managers in Offshore Centers in India know the techniques to successfully hire, train, and lead their technical team members to deliver excellent results on their projects, even if these technical personnel are not as highly experienced as their U.S. counterparts.

An Offshore Center manager was reporting to an engineering director in the HO. The HO director asked the Offshore Center manager to hire *senior* technical persons for the projects—personnel with experience similar to that of senior technical persons in the HO. The HO director was expecting these technical persons to have at least eight years of experience in the technical domain of the projects of the company.

The Offshore Center manager tried hard to find such professionals in the industry but failed in her efforts for multiple reasons:

- Senior persons with at least eight years experience in the industry in India were generally handling managerial roles and were unwilling to return to technical ladder roles.
- Even if such senior technical professionals were available, their experience was not totally relevant to the technical domain of the projects of the company.
- The HO director had proposed that these professionals should be designated as "senior programmers" as per the U.S. norms. However, technical professionals with such experience in the industry in India already had fancy designations, such as "assistant manager," "project leader," "technical leader," etc. These professionals were unwilling to apply for the job opportunity because the designation of "senior programmer" was unattractive to them, and it sounded like a demotion.

Thus, the Offshore Center manager wanted the HO director to relax the hiring criteria by allowing hiring of professionals with lesser experience but with all the experience being relevant to the technical domain of the company. These young professionals would not currently have any fancy designation and would be willing to accept the "senior programmer" designation.

However, the HO Director was inflexible and refused to relax the hiring criteria, since he feared that less experienced technical persons might not be able to deliver successfully on the projects.

In desperation, the Offshore Center manager used an ingenious way to satisfy the HO director: She hired technical professionals with at least eight years experience, but with only half, or less, of their experience being relevant to the company's technical domain! Since these professionals were now getting opportunities to work on more complex technologies and projects, they did not mind their new designations.

Interestingly, the HO director was quite satisfied with this convoluted approach. He was only concerned with the requisite experience levels of the employees. Since all these new hires had at least eight years technical experience, the HO director felt confident that they were experienced enough to deliver on the projects.

However, this hiring approach was obviously not the best option for the Offshore Center. The Center was now incurring a high salary cost for senior employees with largely irrelevant experience in the technical domain of their projects. The project execution costs increased while the output was low, leading to low profit margins for the company.

Solution

The HO director should have realized that the Offshore Center manager is experienced enough to effectively hire and manage her team to deliver on the projects. The HO director should have insisted only on the Offshore Center team delivering the expected results on the projects and should not have dictated the approach to be followed by the Offshore Center manager.

The Offshore Center manager would then have flexibility to hire a team with appropriate experience to deliver on the project. The Offshore Center manager should have also been given the flexibility to decide the designations of the employees, as per the norms prevalent in their country.

The Offshore Center manager would have then hired professionals with three or four years experience, but with all their experience being totally relevant to the technical domain of the projects. These professionals would have been much less costly to the company but would have still performed at par with the senior professionals who were hired with at least eight years of experience, but who had almost half their experience in areas irrelevant to the company's projects.

The flexibility on deciding the designations of the employees would have also allowed the Offshore Center manager to hire some core senior professionals for the team, by attracting them with fancy designations.

The Offshore Center manager would then have been able to lead a strong team who would have delivered successfully on their projects, with high saving on project costs.

4.3. Downsize with Consideration to Local Sensitivities

Global companies sometimes resort to downsizing their teams to counter financial downturns. Since this phenomenon may be quite common in such companies, it may not be a sensitive issue for their employees. Employees realize that the possibility of being retrenched, under extreme circumstances, is a stark reality. They are prepared to face such a reality and make alternative plans for their future career.

Such a global company, however, may be running an Offshore Center in a country where retrenchment of employees may not be an acceptable norm. The phenomenon could be rare, and there could also be a social stigma attached to someone being fired from his or her job. It is also possible that some companies in that country may even have inhibitions about hiring professionals fired from their previous employers, suspecting that the reasons for retrenchment could have been nonperformance of the professional rather than strategic downsizing in the previous employer company. Hence, the Offshore Center employees could be sensitive to the issue of employee retrenchment.

Local companies in the country of the Offshore Center avoid downsizing by taking multiple precautions:

- The companies hire quite conservatively, taking into consideration long-term expected future business to justify any hiring.
- They manage temporary financial downturns by resorting to across-the-board salary cuts, rather than reducing the employee count.
- They use employee retrenchment only as a last resort, if there seems to be absolutely no possibility of financial recovery for the company in the long term.

The HO management of a company running an Offshore Center in such a country should demonstrate concern for such local sensitivities to downsizing. They should even be careful of issuing statements or giving presentations that can be misunderstood because of the sensitivities of the Offshore Center employees.

In fact, even simple innocuous statements should be reworded as per the local sensitivities of the Offshore Center. For example, a standard human resources (HR) presentation on "employee lifecycle" titled "Hire to Fire" may have to be changed to "Hire to Exit" before being presented to the Offshore Center employees!

In the event of a financial crisis in the company that requires cost cutting in the Offshore Center, first an effort should be made to cut costs under various budget headings, without the need for downsizing. For example, the Offshore Center can reduce the business travel of its employees and instead use more tele-conferencing to meet the travel objectives; it can reduce some employee perks and benefits; and it can even agree to across-the-board salary cuts for a limited period until the financial crisis passes. Such a strategy may avoid the need for retrenchment of employee count.

However, if the financial crisis persists for long time, then such an extreme situation can make downsizing in the Offshore Center unavoidable. Even then, however, the process of downsizing should be conducted in a sensitive manner. It must be ensured that the Offshore Center employees are not emotionally impacted on being retrenched, and that their future career prospects in their country are also not adversely impacted.

Such compassionate acts will make the company win the faith of its remaining employees in the Offshore Center. The company will also then not lose its credibility among other professionals in the Offshore Center country. These professionals will be interested in joining the company in its future hiring exercises, post the financial crisis.

Case Study 4.2

A U.S.-based product development company was developing multiple products and was running an Offshore Center in India. Each product was being developed by a separate division in the HO, and each of these divisions had a counterpart division, and a corresponding team, in the Offshore Center. All the divisions were reporting to the vice president for engineering in the HO.

Unfortunately, for business reasons, the company decided to close down one of these product divisions globally. It was decided to retrench all the employees in that product division in the Offshore Center.

Employees in India are quite sensitive to being retrenched, worried that it may create a negative impression about them with prospective future employers, and fear that even if some employers offer them jobs they would have absolutely no negotiating power left to demand their deserved compensation.

The vice president understood and appreciated these sensitivities of the Offshore Center employees. He was aware that the employees might have problems finding new jobs and decided to go out of his way to assist them out in this endeavor.

The vice president had friends in top management positions in some U.S. companies working in the same technology domain as the product division that was being closed. He contacted them to explore whether they had options within their India Offshore Centers for these retrenched employees. He learned that one of these companies had recently set up an India Offshore Center and was desperately looking to hire professionals with expertise in its technology domain. The vice president shared the profiles of the retrenched team with that company, and they enthusiastically agreed to hire *all* of them.

The vice president struck a deal with that company to protect the interests of his retrenched employees. That company agreed to hire these employees by giving them salary protection, and also offering them stock options equivalent to ones they were getting earlier.

The employees were happy that their interests had been protected because of these efforts of the vice president. Further, with this act of going the extra step to help its downsized employees, the company's Offshore Center earned a lot of goodwill from other professionals in India. These professionals were more than willing to join the Offshore Center in its future recruitment requirements.

4.4. Share the Pain

The Offshore Center and the HO are generally in distant countries in different time zones, with time difference being even in the range of half a day. The project teams in the Offshore Center and the HO need to interact regularly through conference calls for discussions about their closely interlinked projects. One major sensitivity issue for employees of the Offshore Center is the impact on their work–life balance because of the time-zone difference in these teleconferences.

If these interlocation teleconferences are *always* held in the daytime of the HO and late evening/night time of the Offshore Center, it can create negative emotions in the Offshore Center employees. The Offshore Center employees' personal lives suffer because they must work at what are for them odd hours. They may also believe that the HO is being unfair to them by making them endure these hardships regularly.

The HO teams must learn to be sensitive to such concerns of the Offshore Center employees. The best option for handling this issue is for the teams in both locations to agree to "share the pain." They should agree to hold about half the meetings during the daytime of the HO, and the rest of the meetings during the daytime of the Offshore Center. Thus, the negative impact on the work–life balance of the Offshore Center teams will be halved, and they will also appreciate the fact that the HO teams are being fair to them.

These problems occurring due to the difference in time zones of different offices become more complex if the company has multiple Offshore Centers across the globe, each in a widely different time zone. It then becomes quite difficult to schedule meeting times that will be convenient to all the offices (see Case Study 4.3). An interesting ground rule for handling such situations might be that if you are unable to find a meeting time that is convenient to all the locations, then choose a meeting time that is *equally inconvenient* to all the locations, rather than choosing a time that is *always* convenient to only one of the locations!

Case Study 4.3

A product development company was executing a large project that was distributed across its U.S. HO and its India Offshore Center. The project was for development of a core product of the company. The project modules across these locations had a number of interdependencies. The project managers in both locations needed to communicate regularly to resolve them. Hence, the project managers in the HO and the Offshore Center held teleconferences twice a week to resolve their dependencies and make key project decisions.

The overall project was headed by an engineering director in the HO. He, along with the project managers in the HO and the Offshore Center, was part of these meetings. The product specifications for which the project was being executed were decided by a product manager, who was also generally included in these meetings. A program manager was responsible for planning the project release, resolving local and interlocation dependencies, resource planning and procurement, etc. She was responsible for conducting these meetings, and hence was a part of the meetings.

The number of project managers working on the project was almost equal in the HO and the Offshore Center locations. However, since the director, the product manager, and the program manager were all based in the HO, the total number of participants in the meetings was always higher in the HO than in the Offshore Center. It was only on rare occasions that the number of participants from the Offshore Center was higher, which generally happened only when the meetings were focused mostly on resolving the interdependencies of the Offshore Center project modules that required the participation of only the involved HO project managers.

The director decided that the meeting time should be such that it would be convenient to the *majority* of the participants in the meeting. Hence, most of the meetings were being held in the daytime of the HO. Thus, the Offshore Center managers had to participate regularly in meetings during their late evening time, leading to a lot of resentment among them. These odd hours of working started impacting their personal lives badly. They perceived the director to be unfair to them, and they thought he was showing bias toward his local HO teams.

The Offshore Center managers protested to the director, who finally corrected himself by holding alternate meetings in the daytime of each location. The Offshore Center managers were satisfied with this new arrangement.

However, this reprieve was quite short-lived, because the company then bought another small company at yet another location. The product of that acquired company also had to be integrated into the ongoing project. Hence, the director decided to include the project managers of that location also in these meetings.

Unfortunately, these three offices were spread across the globe. It was practically impossible to find a meeting time that would not result in at least one location's participants having to attend the meeting from around 11:30 p.m. onward in their local time.

Although one out of every three meetings was now being held in the daytime of each one of the locations, the meetings were still quite inconvenient to many participants. The participants of at least one of the locations were attending meetings that started at 11:30 p.m., and its managers wanted to be released quickly from the meeting. Hence, *all* the meetings seemed to end within half-an-hour's time to avoid too much discomfort to the participants attending at their late night time. The purpose of the meetings was becoming defeated, as the discussions were not sufficiently thorough. Most of the project decisions were now being made without much participation and input from the involved stakeholders, which did not auger well for the project.

Solution

The meetings involving all three locations did not require the participation of all the managers in all these locations. Instead, a better option would have been for the program manager in the HO to accept responsibility for collecting and sharing information between different locations. She could have held separate meetings with each of the locations at convenient times for those locations. The managers in the location would attend these meetings and share detailed information about their project progress, interdependencies to be resolved, clarifications desired from stakeholders in other locations, project decisions required for them to progress further on their projects, etc.

The program manager should have then shared the information gathered from these meetings with other locations, including the HO. She would then be representing the complete management team of a location in the meeting and would be able to share project progress details, resolve interdependencies with other locations, and provide the necessary input required by the HO decision makers to make the right and informed decisions.

There would probably still be some critical project issues or interdependencies that could only be resolved by a meeting of the respective project managers, since the program manager would not have the needed deep insight into the project. To resolve these very critical interdependencies, the respective project managers in different locations would still have to attend late-night meetings. However, since the discussion in these meetings would focus on only a small number of critical issues, the meetings could generally be easily completed in the usual half-hour meeting duration.

Thus, these acts of the program manager would allow all the project objectives to be met with minimal impact on the work–life balance of the managers in various locations.

4.5. Local Management Committee to Decide Offshore Center Norms

Companies should realize that the managers in the Offshore Center are the most knowledgeable about the work culture, management practices, processes, career growth aspirations, employee designations, and employee sensitivities in their country. In comparison, the HO management team is based in a different country with limited knowledge of the norms of the country of the Offshore Center. Companies should, hence, give freedom for making decisions about the norms to be followed in the Offshore Center to the local managers, since they are best equipped to handle this responsibility.

However, it should still be noted that the projects being executed in the HO and the Offshore Center are closely interlinked. There is a need to integrate the activities in both locations if these projects are to be delivered successfully. This objective should be met by allowing the HO management to apply the HO norms on the Offshore Center *for project management aspects,* such as having similar documentation standards and project delivery processes for execution of projects across both the locations. All the other norms for the Offshore Center should be decided by the local managers.

Offshore Center managers should form a local committee to decide Offshore Center policies and other norms, as per the sensitivities and expectations of the professionals within their country. The following are some of the functions to be performed by the local management committee.

1. Decide the policies, work culture, and management practices of the Offshore Center as per the norms of the country. Although these practices should be decided per local norms, the committee should still be open to adopting some of the best practices of the HO wherever they seem useful and relevant.

2. Decide the career growth norms and the local designations of the Offshore Center employees as per the prevalent norms in their country. The employees will then be happy they are getting similar career growth, roles, and designations as their peers in the industry in their country.

   The HO management will have decided the global designations of the employees of the Offshore Center, as per the HO norms. The Offshore Center local management committee should decide the mapping of the local designations of the employees to their global designations. The employees will then have dual designations, each designation clearly defining their position in the local and global hierarchy.

3. Act as a buffer between the HO management and the local Offshore Center employees. If the HO management makes any decision for the company as a whole, the Offshore Center local management committee should evaluate the decision, study its relevance to the local norms being followed in their country, analyze whether the decision might have a negative impact on the morale of the Offshore Center employees, and then refine the decision as per local norms before implementing the decision for the Offshore Center employees. Thus, the aim should be to implement

the decision as per the requirements of the company, but still refine it to make it suitable and palatable to the Offshore Center employees.

Similarly, any major communication from the HO management for the Offshore Center employees should be vetted by the Offshore Center local management committee and refined as per the sensitivities of the employees. It will then ensure proper messaging to the Offshore Center employees and avoid any possibility of the message being interpreted negatively by them.

4. Work closely with the HO managers and teams to sensitize them about the expectations and sensitivities of the Offshore Center employees. Thus, the HO teams will then learn to be cautious in their words and actions when dealing with the Offshore Center employees.

These techniques will allow the Offshore Center to integrate with the HO but still retain its location-specific identity and character. The techniques will help meet the growth expectations and aspirations of the Offshore Center employees, which will motivate them to perform to their full potential.

* * * * *

It is a known fact that Offshore Centers have many highly capable managers and technical personnel who deserve to reach top management and top technical positions in the global hierarchy of the company. However, in many companies, the global top positions are filled mostly by HO employees. The Offshore Center employees rarely get opportunities to rise to such positions because of constraints due to their not being based in the HO location. Chapter 5 will analyze the constraints faced by Offshore Center employees in reaching for such top positions. The chapter will suggest techniques to overcome these constraints, to allow deserving Offshore Center employees to reach global top positions and make significant contributions to the company.

Chapter 5

Career Growth for Offshore Center Employees to Global Top Positions

Offshore Centers have many senior and highly capable managers and technical personnel. These professionals deserve to reach top management and top technical positions in the global hierarchy of the company. If they reach such positions, they can make significant contributions to the global company, and to the Offshore Center.

However, it has been observed that the global top positions of companies are filled mostly by head office (HO) employees. Offshore Center employees rarely get opportunities to rise to such positions because of constraints they face, especially since they are not based in the HO location. Offshore Center employees generally handle limited roles and responsibilities, with minimal exposure to external entities, since they are not based in the HO. Such limited exposure does not prepare them for being considered for the global top positions, compared to the vast responsibilities being handled by employees within the HO. Thus, companies lose out on the contributions of highly capable Offshore Center professionals, who could add significant value if they were to handle top management and technical roles.

This chapter suggests techniques that will allow career growth of senior Offshore Center employees to key global top positions based purely on their merit and not constrained by their location. The chapter starts by discussing the need for highly deserving Offshore Center employees to reach the company's global top positions, by highlighting the considerable value they can add to the company. It then analyzes the constraints faced by Offshore Center employees in reaching these global top positions. It suggests the role to be played by HO senior management in grooming Offshore Center employees to be considered for global top positions, by offering them responsibilities that their HO counterparts normally handle. Further, the chapter recommends the need to have balanced composition of selection committees and a fair selection process to decide the career growth of employees to global top positions, without any bias for or against their location. The chapter concludes by recommending against the practice in some companies of creating a *quota* for Offshore Center employees in company's global top positions, since such a strategy can weaken the company's global top management and technical teams. The chapter, instead, stresses the need to groom the Offshore Center employees effectively so they can be considered, and selected, for global top positions based purely on their merit, without the need for any quota.

5.1. Need for Deserving Offshore Center Employees to Reach Global Top Positions

A company must realize that highly capable professionals are available in all its locations—in its HO and in its Offshore Centers. Highly capable Offshore Center professionals should get full opportunities to rise to the global top positions of the company, even to the global CEO position. Location should not be a constraint for capable employees.

Unfortunately, in a large number of companies, only employees in the HO get opportunities to rise to global top positions, by virtue of their being located within the HO. Offshore Center employees rarely reach the company's top management and technical positions, such as CEO, vice president for engineering, CTO, chief architect, etc.

A company, for its own good, must ensure that its global top management and technical teams consist of its most capable employees, who can make the right strategic decisions for the company's success. The company's own interests are harmed if highly capable professionals from the Offshore Center do not reach global top positions, and these positions are instead filled by comparatively less capable HO professionals, purely by virtue of their location. Companies then fail to capitalize on the full potential of its highly capable employees, which can result in potential loss of revenues to the company.

Further, if highly capable and deserving Offshore Center professionals fail to be promoted to global top positions and less capable HO professionals reach these positions instead, then the best Offshore Center professionals become demoralized. They may think the company is being unfair to them, and that they are not getting the career growth they deserve. Such demoralization can negatively impact their productivity and their contributions to the company. In extreme cases, they may even quit the company to join another company that offers them such global career growth. Since these key professionals are the backbone of the Offshore Center, the productivity and deliverables from the center suffer greatly.

The Offshore Center senior management should convince the HO top management of the need to promote Offshore Center managers to global top management positions, and senior technical persons to global top technical positions. The Offshore Center senior management should impress upon the HO that by being promoted to such global top positions, these professionals can use their extensive expertise to make highly successful strategic decisions that can add significantly to the revenues of the company. Further, these professionals will also be able to represent the interests of the Offshore Center in the top management team and can make decisions to run large and critical projects/activities within the Offshore Center, leading to much higher cost savings for the company. The Offshore Center senior management must also stress the fact that if the Offshore Center managers/technical architects grow to global top positions, it will significantly enhance the morale of all the Offshore Center employees, who will strive to reach similar goals. Hence, overall Offshore Center productivity will increase, adding to the company's revenues and profits.

5.2. Constraints to Global Career Growth of Offshore Center Employees

The core reason why Offshore Center employees do not reach global top positions is that their jobs and responsibilities in the Offshore Center do not prepare them for handling top management and technical roles. They play limited roles because of the constraints of being based in the Offshore Center, while their counterparts in the HO handle much wider roles and responsibilities.

The top management and technical personnel of the company are expected to make the strategic decisions for the company, which can have far reaching consequences for the future of the company. Some of the responsibilities they handle are choosing the right strategies for the future of the company; visualizing new and potentially highly successful products to be developed by the company (in the case of product development companies); and deciding new business domains in which to invest heavily to win high-revenue services projects from clients in the future (in the case of services companies).

All these responsibilities can be handled only by professionals who have gained deep understanding of:

- The company's existing strategies concerning its products and services offerings
- The company's business and technical domains of work
- Markets for the company's products and services
- Requirements of the key and high-revenue-generating customers of the company
- Offerings of the competition, etc.

Thus, to be considered for a top management or technical role, the Offshore Center employees need to work closely with the HO management team to achieve various purposes:

- Work closely with the current top management and technical personnel *in the HO* to become deeply aware of thought process behind deciding the current strategies of the company.
- Interact closely with the marketing teams *in the HO* to get exposure to the markets for the company's products and services.
- Gain experience of interacting closely with the key customers of the company, who are generally based *in the country of the HO.*
- Work closely with the product management teams *in the HO* to understand the offerings of the competition.
- Learn from product management the process of product conceptualization and planning, etc.

The above objectives can mostly be met if the employee is based within the HO, which allows him or her to interact regularly with the top management, marketing teams, key customers, product management teams, etc. Unfortunately, the Offshore Center employees are based at a distance to all these entities and cannot interact regularly with these entities to gain the necessary exposure required in all these aspects.

Further, even if the Offshore Center employees do acquire, over a period of time, some exposure to the products and services of the company, the duration of the exposure will still be less than that of their HO counterparts.

Most senior professionals in the HO have been working on the company's products and services for many years and hence are quite knowledgeable about them. In contrast, the Offshore Center is generally set up late in the company's life cycle, and its employees may have much less experience with the products and services of the company.

The company would be taking a major risk in promoting its senior Offshore Center professionals to the global top positions without their first having a greater understanding of the company's strategic goals and objectives, its products, and services.

5.3. Grooming Offshore Center Employees for Global Top Positions

All the above assertions show that the constraints faced because of being based in the Offshore Center may make it difficult for its deserving and capable employees to reach global top positions. To achieve this career growth objective, the Offshore Center employees need to gain more in-depth knowledge of the company's strategies, customers, markets, competition, products, and services, similar to that of their counterparts in the HO.

However, if the Offshore Center has exceptionally bright professionals, they will have the talent to pick up such knowledge fast. The senior management team in the HO must take on the responsibility for grooming these Offshore Center professionals for global top positions through multiple means:

- Regularly mentoring and training these Offshore Center employees on the company's strategies, technologies, products, services, markets, etc.
- Offloading to them more complex tasks to allow them to hone their skills.
- Offering them slowly increasing higher responsibilities, including closer interactions with the HO product management teams and key customers, to prepare them for the challenges of the top positions, etc.

Thus, the aim of the HO senior management should be to prepare the Offshore Center employees for global career growth by exposing them to opportunities currently available only within the HO.

Let us consider the example of a product development company. Currently the project managers and architects within the HO get involved with a new product development starting almost from the time the product is conceptualized by the product management. They then get opportunities to interact closely with key stakeholders, such as the product management team and key customers, to gain insight into the need for the product, to learn how the product can exceed the capabilities of competing products, and to learn how various critical needs of key customers can be leveraged into features of the product. Thus, they not only have a complete understanding of the product but also recognize how the company's product strategies are decided and executed.

In contrast, the project managers and architects in the Offshore Center are involved in the product development process late in the cycle, after the product has been conceptualized, planned, product specifications formalized, and the overall architecture finalized. The Offshore Center management and architects are then assigned the responsibilities for designing and implementing *just some modules* of the product. Thus, they lack overall understanding of the product, its vision, and strategies.

The HO senior management should start including the Offshore Center managers and architects in the process of product development at the same time as their HO counterparts. These Offshore Center professionals will then get opportunities to work closely with the key stakeholders in the HO, to gain a deeper understanding of the company's strategies, markets, competition, product vision, etc. Thus, they will eventually be as ready to be considered for the company's global top positions as their HO counterparts.

However, it should be noted that the above objectives can be met only if the Offshore Center professionals work closely with various stakeholders in the HO. They may need to interact regularly with these stakeholders, including in face-to-face meetings with them. The Offshore Center professionals are based in a different country, which can make it difficult to meet this objective. It is not always practical to base these professionals in the HO for long periods or to schedule frequent travel to the HO to meet these objectives. Such exercises will defeat the basic purpose of basing employees in an Offshore Center. Instead, the HO senior management should think of some *short-term assignments* for the Offshore Center professionals that allow them to interact for short periods with the stakeholders in the HO but still give them the requisite knowledge and insight required to become prepared for top management and technical roles. One such possible assignment is discussed in Case Study 5.2.

5.4. Fair Selection Process

Companies should also ensure that they provide a fair assessment and selection process to select the right employees for the global top positions. The selection process should take into consideration the differences in working in the HO and in the Offshore Center, and should have unbiased performance assessment norms for the Offshore Center employees and those in the HO. The parameters on which the assessment is based should not include accomplishments on tasks that can only be performed by being located in the HO.

Further, companies must create truly representative global selection committees to decide employee selection to global top positions. The committees must have representation from the Offshore Center, who can ensure fair assessment of the Offshore Center employees against the competing HO employees.

Sometimes, some complex reporting structures within the company can weaken the case for Offshore Center employees in such selection committee meetings. Case Study 5.1 presents one such example and suggests a method to overcome such problems.

5.5. Avoid a Common Pitfall

Previous sections have so far considered the case of companies not giving enough opportunities to Offshore Center employees for them to reach the global top positions. These sections have suggested techniques to overcome these constraints. However, there are also some companies that, in their effort to be *overly fair* to their Offshore Center employees, take the other extreme position. These companies give special consideration to Offshore Center senior employees by creating a "quota" for them in the global top management and technical positions, regardless of these employees being capable or being fully ready for these roles.

This option can be quite detrimental to the company, since the professionals at the top management and technical positions decide the company's strategies and growth plans. They are effectively deciding the future of the company. If some of the professionals at these top positions have not reached these positions on merit, they may make poor decisions that severely impact the future of the company.

For example, a professional from the Offshore Center who does not possess a deep understanding of the markets for the company's products may reach a top management position that decides on future products to be developed by the company. He or she may then make an erroneous decision to invest heavily in a new line of products that has very low revenue potential. The consequences of such a decision can be disastrous for the company.

Thus, companies should avoid creating quotas for the Offshore Center employees in their global top positions. They should, instead, create opportunities for Offshore Center employees to gain the requisite knowledge to be prepared to perform such critical roles, using the techniques suggested in the previous sections.

Case Study 5.1

The highest technical grade in a large global product company was the "Fellow" grade. Only the top eight to ten technical personnel in the whole company reached this grade. The Fellows, as a group, were responsible for deciding the overall technical strategies of the company. Hence they were effectively deciding the future of the company.

The company was developing multiple products. The decision on promotions to the Fellow grade was made by a Selection Committee consisting of the current Fellows and the vice presidents for engineering of each of the product divisions.

The company had been running an Offshore Center for almost a decade, but no one from there had ever been promoted to the Fellow grade. The Offshore Center had a very capable technical architect. Over the years he had demonstrated that he was technically more capable than his counterpart architects in the HO, including even some of the current Fellows. His name had been put forward to the selection committee repeatedly for promotion to the Fellow grade, but the committee invariably rejected his case, year after year.

The Offshore Center had multiple teams, each dedicated to an individual product. The final reporting of each of these teams was to the respective vice president for engineering for that product in the HO. The architect was reporting to an engineering director in the Offshore Center, who was in turn reporting

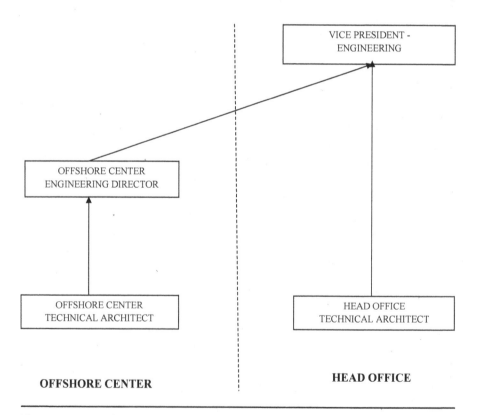

Figure 5-1　Interlocation reporting structure.

to the product vice president in the HO (see Figure 5-1). The reason for rejection of the Offshore Center architect was not his merit, but a peculiar situation created by this reporting structure.

The architect belonged to an Offshore Center product team whose HO counterpart team had no Fellow among them. The HO counterpart team for the product also had an architect who had been considered for promotion to the Fellow grade for many years. The HO architect was reporting directly to the vice president.

Each time the Offshore Center architect's promotion was considered by the selection committee, the HO architect was also being simultaneously considered. The Offshore Center architect's case was supposed to be "sponsored" by his product vice president, because the selection committee had no representative from the Offshore Center.

However, the product vice president wanted his own HO architect to be promoted to Fellow grade first, since overall product development was controlled from the HO. Hence, in the selection meetings the product vice president would invariably end up raising the case of the HO architect first, and more strongly, compared to the case of the Offshore Center architect.

The selection committee would then vote out the case of the Offshore Center architect, since the proposer himself was not raising the case of the candidate strongly.

These repeated rejections made the Offshore Center architect feel dejected, and he was even contemplating quitting the company. However, one year the HO architect got the requisite votes from the selection committee and was promoted to Fellow grade. *The very next year,* the Offshore Center architect got promoted to Fellow grade by winning the *maximum* number of votes from the selection committee, based on his credentials. Interestingly, despite having the same credentials, his case had been rejected for years!

The reason was simple: This was the first time the product vice president had sincerely promoted the credentials of the Offshore Center architect in the selection committee meeting and had supported his case strongly, since he no longer had to push the case of the HO architect.

Hence, even though the Offshore Center architect had the best credentials among all the Fellow candidates, he was not promoted for years, purely because of the organization reporting structure and the faulty composition of the selection committee. In fact, an obvious consequence of this reporting structure could have been that if the HO architect had never been promoted to the Fellow position, then the Offshore Center architect would also have never reached the position, since his case would have never been supported strongly by the product vice president! The company would then have completely lost the services of a deserving Fellow, who had the capability to add significant value to the company.

Solution

The composition of the selection committee was faulty in that all its members were from the HO—all the product vice presidents were based in the HO, and all the current Fellows were from the HO. The aim of the company was to give fair representation to all the product divisions of the company by including each of their vice presidents on the committee. However, the company had overlooked the fact that *all* these vice presidents belonged to the HO, and the Offshore Center was left totally unrepresented in the committee.

The selection committee should have had fair representation from the Offshore Center, by including all the engineering directors from the Offshore Center who were responsible for developing various products. Thus, the Offshore Center director to whom the Offshore Center architect was directly reporting would have been a member of the selection committee. The Offshore Center director would have then supported the case of the Offshore Center architect much more strongly in the selection meeting. This action by the Offshore Center director would have created a level playing field between the Offshore Center architect and the HO architect (and other candidates being considered for the Fellow position) in the selection meeting, and only the more meritorious among them would have been promoted first.

Thus, the Offshore Center Architect would have been promoted to the Fellow grade much earlier. Since he was a highly capable technical professional, he could have contributed much sooner to deciding the company's new technical strategies, which could have resulted in creation of future products that could have generated huge revenues for the company.

Further, faster promotion of the Offshore Center architect to the Fellow grade would have motivated other Offshore Center architects to work hard toward reaching the same goal. Their efforts and contributions would have increased significantly, leading to much higher success in projects being executed in the Offshore Center.

Case Study 5.2

A global product company had been running an Offshore Center for many years. The core tasks of product planning, architecture, and overall project control resided with the HO. The Offshore Center was given only some project modules to be designed and implemented.

The technical directions for the company were deliberated and set by a committee of Fellows. All the current Fellows were from the HO.

The Offshore Center had a very capable architect who, based on his capabilities, was ready to be promoted to the Fellow grade. However, the selection committee never looked favorably at this candidate. The expectations of the company from Fellows were much more than the knowledge gained by merely designing some project modules. The Fellows were responsible for deciding the directions for the future technologies and products for the company. Hence, the Fellows were expected to have deep understanding of overall product strategies, competition offerings, markets, key customers' expectations from the products, etc.

Since the Offshore Center Architect was not based in the HO and had minimal interactions with the product management and other stakeholders, he had very little exposure to these aspects of the products. Hence, his credentials were considered weak by the selection committee, and he was invariably rejected.

Since the Offshore Center had about 30% of the company's total global engineering team, the head of the Offshore Center was insisting on having at least one Fellow from the Offshore Center for fair representation. He requested the company's vice president for engineering to create a quota for the Offshore Center among Fellows. He wanted the Offshore Center architect to be promoted to the Fellow grade under this quota.

The vice president rightly dismissed this request. He understood that Fellows play a very critical role in deciding the future of the company, and they had to have the right expertise, knowledge, and exposure to discharge their responsibilities successfully. The Offshore Center architect was still not ready to take up the responsibility.

The vice president decided to support the Offshore Center architect in the ideal way, by preparing him for the Fellow role. He decided to assign the Offshore Center architect some assignments that would prepare him for the Fellow role. However, the vice president also realized that it would be impractical for the Offshore Center architect to stay for a long period in the HO, and hence a short-term assignment was necessary.

The company had a core product (referred to as its "business solution" for the rest of this case study) for a business domain. This business solution was missing a set of capabilities that the competition was offering. A few start-ups had developed small products that had the missing capabilities desired in the company's business solution. Since developing these product capabilities would have taken considerable time, the company decided to acquire one of these start-ups and integrate its product within its current business solution.

It was decided to form a team of a product manager and a senior technical person to study the products of various start-ups for the following purposes:

- Evaluate which one of these products would have the features that meet the requirements of the key customers of the company.
- Evaluate whether the product would have the features required be able to challenge the features available in business solutions from the competition of the company's business solution.

- Evaluate whether the product would have a robust technical design for large-scale deployment.
- Evaluate the product architecture to judge whether it would allow easy integration with the current business solution of the company.

In the past, the task of technical evaluation of products had traditionally been handled totally from within the HO. The vice president decided to offload this complex and challenging task to the Offshore Center architect, along with a product manager from the HO.

The Offshore Center architect worked closely with the product manager to meet the following objectives:

- Understand the requirements of the key customers of the company from their current business solution.
- Identify the features missing in the business solution.
- Understand the features of similar business solutions being offered by the key competitors of the company.
- Identify and evaluate a set of start-ups that were offering products having the above features desired by their key customers and additional features provided by the competition.

Both of them jointly selected two such start-ups and decided to evaluate them thoroughly for possible acquisition. They made short visits to the offices of these start-ups and met their product management and technical teams to gain deeper insight into their product capabilities, and to gain understanding of the product architecture to evaluate the feasibility of its integration with the current business solution of the company. They also accompanied the teams of these start-ups to key customer sites to evaluate the performance of the actual deployment of their products.

Based on these data, the Offshore Center architect and the product manager made a thorough comparative evaluation of the products of these two start-ups, and finally decided to select one of the start-ups for acquisition. The decision was hailed highly by top management, who could see the high potential of revenue generation from the product of the acquired start-up.

Thus, through this detailed exercise, the Offshore Center architect gained practical understanding about deciding product strategies, interacting with the product management unit, understanding the requirements of key customers, evaluating offerings of the competition, evaluating various products, and making a sound judgment on the right product for the company.

Interestingly, the Offshore Center architect had to make *only two short visits of just a few days each* to the offices of these start-ups (located in the country of the HO) to meet all the above objectives.

These results delivered by the Offshore Center architect held him in good stead during the subsequent meeting of the Fellow selection committee. The committee members appreciated the fact that the Offshore Center architect now had the requisite knowledge, expertise, and experience to be able to perform the responsibilities of being a Fellow. The committee promoted him to the Fellow grade. He then made significant contributions to the future technology and product strategies of the company.

After some years, this Offshore Center Fellow decided to quit the company for personal reasons. Interestingly, the Offshore Center head again raised the argument that since the Offshore Center already held that Fellow post, the replacement for the position must be found by promoting another architect selected from the Offshore Center only, instead of going through the standard selection process!

Needless to say, the vice president politely rejected the request and, instead, initiated another process of grooming the Offshore Center architects for the Fellow position.

* * * * *

Case Study 5.1 discussed the negative impact of not having Offshore Center representation in the selection committee for deciding the promotion of Offshore Center employees to the company's global top positions. Besides such selection committees, companies create a number of other management committees to make company policies and decide on various issues that impact the company as a whole, including the HO and the Offshore Center. A number of companies make the mistake of not having Offshore Center representation, or having ineffective Offshore Center representation, in such management committees. These committees then fail to make decisions in the best interest of the Offshore Center. Such decisions negatively impact Offshore Center employee morale, motivation, and productivity; which then badly impact the deliverables from the Center. Chapter 6 will discuss the need for giving fair representation to the Offshore Center management in these committees by discussing the negative impact on the Offshore Center because of the lack of such representation, and by describing how fair representation can resolve these issues.

Chapter 6

Fair Representation of Offshore Center Management in Global Committees

Companies create a number of management committees to decide various issues that impact the company as a whole, including the head office (HO) and the Offshore Center. Some of these committees may be established to decide overall company policies, management practices, employee appraisal norms, employee benefits, distribution of teams among various locations, resolution of interlocation contention among the employees, selection of employees for global top positions, etc. The decisions made by such committees can have significant impact on the Offshore Center's productivity, growth, and contributions to the company's revenues and profits. Hence, it is critical that these committees have fair representation from the Offshore Center to allow the company to make decisions that may impact the Offshore Center.

Some companies, however, make the mistake of having either only the HO senior managers in such committees or having a bare minimum or ineffective Offshore Center representation. These committees, then, cannot make decisions in the best interest of the Offshore Center, which impacts negatively on employee morale and subsequently deliverables from the Offshore Center.

The last chapter discussed briefly the negative impact of not having Offshore Center representation in the selection committee that decides on promotion of senior technical personnel to the Fellow grade. This chapter discusses the topic of having Offshore Center representation in various global committees in detail. The chapter first describes some typical global management committees created by companies, and the functions performed by such committees. It then discusses the need for representing the Offshore Center fairly in these committees by discussing the negative impact on the Offshore Center if there is a lack of such representation, and showing how fair representation can resolve these issues.

6.1. Global Management Committees

The introduction mentioned some typical global management committees in companies. The following are examples of functions performed by three such committees.

1. **Growth of the Offshore Center.** Companies distribute their projects between the HO and the Offshore Center. Let us consider the example of a company developing multiple products, with each product division being headed by a vice president for engineering in the HO.

   A committee consisting of all these vice presidents meets at the start of each year to plan the distribution of engineering teams among the HO and the Offshore Center for that year. For example, the committee can decide that of the total engineering team of the company, 70% will be based in the HO and 30% will be based in the Offshore Center. This proportion of the engineering team in the Offshore Center can be increased each year, based on striking a balance between the cost savings that are due to offshoring desired by the company and the capabilities of the Offshore Center teams in executing projects of larger sizes. Once these guidelines have been decided, each product division vice president makes an individual decision on distributing the projects related to his or her product among the teams in the HO and the Offshore Center. He or she will ensure that the proportion of the total team size of the projects of his or her product division to be based in the Offshore Center falls broadly within the overall guidelines of the proportion of the total company engineering team to be based in the Offshore Center.

   Thus, this annual decision of the management committee on the guidelines for the proportion of total engineering team size to be based in the Offshore Center is critical for the Center, since all future project allocations and team growth norms for it will be based on these guidelines.

2. **Employee benefits.** The compensation norms for the company's employees differ in the HO and the Offshore Center, as per the economic status of their respective countries. However, companies generally decide on a similar set of employee benefit schemes for all their employees across various locations. The aim is to provide parity to all the company employees with respect to these benefits.

   One example of an employee benefit might be the norm for covering the employee and his or her family under a company-paid health insurance system. The decisions on such human resources (HR) policies and norms are made by a management committee including the HR senior management and related senior management personnel.

3. **Contention resolution.** Contention can sometime arise in companies between different divisions, between different teams, or between the employees in different divisions/teams. These contentions need to be resolved by an independent committee. Companies achieve this objective by creating a contention resolution committee consisting of senior management personnel representing various divisions/teams along with HR representatives.

6.2. Need for Offshore Center Representation in Committees

Most of the committees described above generally consist of only the senior management personnel of the company, for example, personnel at the vice president level (or above) in the global management hierarchy. The reason for this criterion is that since these committees make critical decisions that can have far-reaching impacts on the company, the committee members must be quite experienced, senior, and mature to be able to make such decisions.

Since the overall control of a large number of projects and activities of the Offshore Center rests with the HO management, most of the senior management personnel of the company are based in the HO. The Offshore Center mostly has personnel at the first-line manager level or at an executive level, and very few (if any) personnel at the global vice president level. Thus, personnel from the Offshore Center generally are not included in these committees, resulting in the committees being almost totally dominated by HO employees.

Further, companies sometimes make a mistake in judging what would be the right and fair representation in these committees. Let us consider the case of a product development company with multiple products, as discussed in the last section. The company will think that its committees must have fair

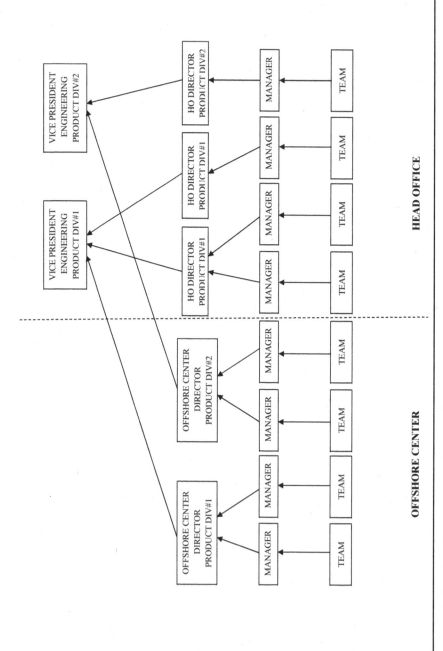

Figure 6-1 Interlocation reporting structure for a multiproduct company.

representation from all the product divisions and hence includes the vice president of each product division in the committee. Since both the HO teams and the Offshore Center teams of a product division finally report to their vice president, it is assumed that the committee composition is fair, since the vice president would represent the viewpoint of both HO and Offshore Center teams of his or her product division in the committee. Hence, the company assumes that it has created a fair committee where Offshore Center views are fully represented.

However, this assumption is not necessarily correct. The teams in the Offshore Center report to their managers/directors in the Center (see Figure 6-1). This Offshore Center management works closely with their teams and has in-depth knowledge of the team members' strengths, expectations, and aspirations. These Offshore Center directors then report to their respective product vice presidents in the HO. The vice presidents in the HO are controlling these Offshore Center teams, but they have limited knowledge about the teams' strengths and expectations because of the distance constraints. With this limited knowledge of the Offshore Center teams, these vice presidents cannot effectively and strongly represent the points of view of the Offshore Center employees in their respective committees. However, they are quite knowledgeable about their local HO teams and hence represent their viewpoints strongly in these committees. Thus, most of the decisions of these committees end up being in favor of the HO, with the Offshore Center not truly getting fair treatment.

Let us consider the example of a committee to determine the growth of the Offshore Center in terms of deciding the proportion of the total company engineering team to be based in the Offshore Center. At the start of the year, the company decides on all the projects to be executed in various technology domains during the year. The committee of the product division vice presidents meets at the start of the year to decide the proposed size of engineering teams in the HO and the Offshore Center to execute these projects.

The vice presidents for each of the product divisions have limited knowledge about the strengths of their Offshore Center teams, although they will be broadly aware of the current expertise in various technology domains of the Offshore Center employees in their respective divisions. Based on this knowledge, they will decide whether projects in various technology domains can be successfully executed in the Offshore Center, and will suggest which projects should be offshored. The total number of projects to be offshored is decided by the committee, along with the proposed overall team size of the Offshore Center for the year in order to execute these projects.

Since the Offshore Center may not currently have employees with expertise in some of the new technology domains in which the company proposes to execute projects, these projects will not be marked for offloading to the

Offshore Center. Thus, only a limited number of projects will be proposed to be offshored, and minimal growth will be planned for the Offshore Center team size. The Offshore Center team size then remains a much smaller proportion of the overall company engineering team size, resulting in lower cost savings for the company.

In contrast to their product division vice presidents, the directors in the Offshore Center are not only knowledgeable about the current expertise of their teams in various technology domains but are also aware of the kind of talent they can recruit from the industry within a short period of time. These directors are aware of the technology domain expertise of employees of similar companies in their location, and they know how to attract these employees to join their Offshore Center. If the concerned committee had also included the directors of various product divisions in the Offshore Center, they would have not only bid for the projects in which their teams already had requisite technology domain expertise, they would also have bid for projects in new technology domains in which they had the confidence to recruit experts from the industry quickly. In the committee meeting, they would have shared details about the available talent in the industry in their location, would have impressed on the committee that they can recruit a large number of employees in the new technology domains of various projects, and would have been able to convince the committee to offload a much larger number of projects to the Offshore Center. Then the company might have decided to significantly grow the Offshore Center team size for the year, resulting in much higher cost savings for the company.

Another example where the presence of Offshore Center representatives can add significant value to the company is in the committee to decide the guidelines for extending various employee benefits across various locations of the company. Let us take the example of deciding whether the company should offer health insurance for the employee and his or her family as an employee benefit. In the country of the HO, extending health insurance benefit may not be a usual norm in the industry. Further, the cost of health insurance may be a high proportion of employee compensation, and the company would have to incur a high cost to extend this benefit to all employees. Thus, if the committee has only HO senior management as members, they will probably decide not to extend this employee benefit. The norm is then applied across all the locations of the company, including the Offshore Center.

However, it may be that the industry norms for various employee benefits in the country of the Offshore Center are quite different from the norms in the country of the HO. In the country of the Offshore Center, most of the competing companies may offer health insurance benefits to employees and their families. Further, in that country the premium for health insurance may be only a paltry sum and a small proportion of employee compensation. If the company decides not to offer the health insurance benefit to employees in the Offshore Center, it will make it difficult for the Offshore Center to attract new hires from competing companies, as these employees will not want to lose their ongoing health insurance benefit to join a new company. Thus, the Offshore Center will have problems hiring excellent talent, which will negatively impact the productivity of the center.

On the other hand, if the committee concerned includes a representative from the Offshore Center, for example, the Offshore Center HR head, then he or she will be quite knowledgeable about the norms in the industry in his or her country. The HR head will be able to share with the rest of the committee the differences in extending health insurance benefits in the HO and in the Offshore Center. He or she may be able to convince the committee that the cost of implementing a health insurance benefit in the Offshore Center is insignificant compared to the cost of implementing one in the HO. He or she might also highlight the possible problems in hiring excellent talent in the absence of this employee benefit, since most of the competing companies in the country of the Offshore Center do offer this benefit. The committee might then have agreed to determine its employee benefits as per the requirements of each location, and might have offered a health insurance benefit to Offshore Center employees. Thus, the Offshore Center representation would have allowed the committee to make decisions in the best interest of the Center.

Similarly, if a committee needs to resolve contentions among the employees of the HO and the Offshore Center, then it must have fair representation from both locations, with members who can effectively put across the point of view of employees of each location. The company might assume that since the vice president of each product division represents his or her division's teams in both locations, he or she can fairly perform this role of his or her division in the committee meetings. However, the vice president is at a distance from the Offshore Center and may not be as knowledgeable about the concerns and expectations of the Offshore Center employees, as he or she primarily is aware of the HO employees close to him or her. Thus, in the committee meetings to resolve a contention between an HO employee and an Offshore Center employee, the vice president may not be able to put across the Offshore Center employee viewpoint strongly, *not because of any bias or ill-intent,* but purely because he or she lacks in-depth knowledge of the Offshore Center employee's psyche, thinking, and concerns. The committee decisions may then end up being heavily weighted in favor of the HO employees rather than the Offshore Center employees, resulting in lack of trust of the Offshore Center employees in the fairness of the committee.

Thus, the committee must have strong representation from the Offshore Center to put across the viewpoints of the Offshore Center employees in the meetings. The Offshore Center employees will then get fair treatment in committee meetings, and the decisions will be in their favor if their stand was right in their contention with the HO employees.

Of course, there are cases in which a vice president in the HO has developed deep understanding of the psyche, needs, and aspirations of the Offshore Center employees of his or her division. He or she will then represent the points of view of the Offshore Center employees strongly in committee meetings and will often win favorable decisions for them. The company may then decide to keep only that vice president in the committee and may not feel the need to have an Offshore Center representative as well. However, even if the vice president is totally fair to his or her division's Offshore Center employees, any decision of the company not to have a separate representative from the Offshore Center in the committee will still be wrong. Companies must make note of the aphorism: *"Not only must Justice be done; it must also be seen to be done."*

Regardless of the intent of the vice president, the Offshore Center employees will still perceive this vice president as *belonging to the HO*, which is an unavoidable fact. The Offshore Center employees will not feel comfortable about their contentions with HO employees being resolved by a committee that has no members from the Offshore Center. Even if the vice president argues the Offshore Center employees' case strongly in the committee's meetings, an employee may still lose his or her case if he or she was in the wrong, and the HO employee with whom he or she had the contention was genuinely right. If such a decision is made, then the Offshore Center employees may simply assume that the decision went against the Offshore Center employee because the committee lacked Offshore Center members who could have made fair decisions for them. Thus, the committee must have representation from the Offshore Center, regardless of the good intent and fairness of the HO members of the committee.

It should be noted that not only should the committees have members from the Offshore Center, the companies should also be careful to choose the right people from the Offshore Center for the purpose. The person selected must be senior, experienced, and mature enough to argue and win his or her viewpoint against the HO senior management team in the committee, who will generally be much more senior and at much higher positions in the company's global hierarchy compared to the Offshore Center personnel. Case Study 6.1 shows that having a junior-level Offshore Center representative in a committee may be only as good as not having any Offshore Center representation in the committee.

Case Study 6.1

A global company had set up an Offshore Center. The company was developing multiple products, with each product division being headed by its respective vice president for engineering in the HO. The Offshore Center teams were executing projects to develop various modules of these products.

The company had traditionally been resolving contentions between its employees through a Contention Resolution Committee consisting of the vice president for HR and the vice president for engineering of each product division. Although all these committee members belonged to the HO, the company did not feel the need to change the composition of the committee after it set up the Offshore Center. The company believed that the respective vice presidents for engineering are the overall heads of their teams, including the Offshore Center teams, and can protect the interests of the employees in all the locations.

The committee had earlier been able to successfully resolve the contentious issues between employees in the HO to the satisfaction of all the employees. In case of a contention between two employees (or a set of employees), the committee would evaluate which of the employee's action was more aligned to his or her work responsibilities and to the goals of the company, and would rule in his or her favor. However, with the addition of an Offshore Center, the dynamics of employee contention had changed. The company soon realized that the existing contention resolution mechanisms of the committee were not geared to resolve contentious issues between different locations.

For example, a typical case of contention between the managers in the Offshore Center and the HO was the repeated attempts of managers in the HO to push all the low-end and uninspiring *maintenance projects* for the existing products to the managers (and their teams) in the Offshore Center, instead of offshoring challenging and high-value projects of developing new products.

The typical reasoning offered by an HO manager pushing the maintenance projects to the Offshore Center was that he or she could then free his or her HO team, who had been working on these projects for some time, and move them to more challenging new product development projects. He or she argued that otherwise he or she feared attrition of these employees, since they were losing their motivation, having been working on uninteresting and nonchallenging projects for a long time.

The impacted Offshore Center manager made efforts to push back these projects. He or she also had similar reasoning for this action—his or her team members would feel demotivated if they worked on uninspiring maintenance projects and that might result in employee attrition.

Hence, even though both the HO and the Offshore Center managers were working toward fulfilling their individual work responsibilities and were working toward achieving the company goal of employee motivation and attrition control, *for their respective locations,* contention still arose.

The committee had not had experience handling such contentious issues earlier, where none of the contending parties seemed to be wrong. Hence, the committee decided that it would need representation from the Offshore Center to resolve such issues. The Offshore Center representative would have an in-depth understanding of the strengths, expectations, aspirations, and concerns of the Offshore Center employees and could best argue their viewpoints in the committee meetings, to get a positive resolution despite such tightly balanced cases of contentions between the employees of the two locations.

The committee thought that since resolving contentions between employees is basically an HR issue, the committee should have a representative from the HR department of the Offshore Center. Since the Offshore Center was still small in size, it had not recruited a senior HR management team but only had some HR executives handling the HR requirements. One of these HR executives was now included in the committee.

Unfortunately, the Offshore Center HR executive was quite junior, and lacked experience and maturity. Based on these limitations, this person was unable to put across the viewpoint of the Offshore Center employees comprehensively in the committee meetings. His arguments were not cogent and were not backed by required data and reasoning.

Further, the person was quite junior in the overall organization hierarchy. In the committee meetings, he was supposed to argue against the points put forward by the vice president–level personnel from the HO. Instead, this individual was totally overwhelmed because of the presence of such senior management personnel in the meeting and was unable to speak up freely. Sometimes this person even feared reprisals if he said something that was against the views of the HO senior management in the committee meetings.

The result was that when contentions arose between employees of the two locations, the Offshore Center HR executive barely spoke up in the committee meetings or did not make a convincing argument. It was as good as not having this representative in the committee.

Hence, most of the decisions of committee ended up favoring the HO employees even if the viewpoint of the Offshore Center employees seemed reasonable, similar to the case discussed of the contention between managers regarding allocating only maintenance projects to the Offshore Center. The repeated decisions against the Offshore Center employees made them feel that the committee was discriminating against them. They were demotivated, and their performance was impacted negatively.

Solution

The reasoning of the committee that only a representative from the HR department, however inexperienced, could properly represent the case of the Offshore Center employees was not correct. Instead, the committee should have selected a member from the Offshore Center who was as senior, experienced, and mature as the other committee members, so there would be equal standing in the committee, and this member could argue the case of the Offshore Center employees in the committee meetings.

Thus, the committee should have included the Offshore Center head instead of the junior HR representative. The Offshore Center head was a senior person and was ranked at the vice president level in the global organizational hierarchy. He deeply understood the problems and concerns of the Offshore Center employees, and could use his vast experience to make a strong case for them in the committee meetings when these employees had contentions with the HO employees.

He could then have argued the cases of the Offshore Center employees much more strongly in such committees. In the committee meetings, he would have been able to respond strongly to the HO vice presidents, who were his *peers* in the overall organization hierarchy. He would have been able to speak his mind freely, without fear of reprisals. Thus, the presence of the Offshore Center head would have created a level playing field between the contending Offshore Center employees and the HO employees in the committee meetings. The committee would then have been able to obtain a deeper understanding of the viewpoints and concerns of all the contending parties, and would have taken a balanced view and decided only in favor of the employees with the right justification. Thus, the committee would have ruled in favor of Offshore Center employees whenever they had genuine concerns that led to contentions. The Offshore Center employees would then have felt that all locations were being treated justly and fairly by the company.

* * * * *

Section 6.2 discussed the need to convince the HO management to offload a large number of big projects to the Offshore Center, to capitalize fully on the strengths of the Offshore Center teams and achieve high cost savings. However, the HO management in many companies believes that their Offshore Center employees are not capable and experienced enough to execute large, core, and complex projects. Hence, their tendency is to offload only simple, peripheral, and low-value projects to the Offshore Center. The Offshore Center is then contributing low revenues to the company. Chapter 7 will argue that the assumptions made by the HO management about the strengths of the Offshore Center employees are wrong, and will show that Offshore Centers generally possess highly capable and experienced professionals who can execute complex and large projects. The chapter will suggest techniques for the Offshore Center management to convince the HO management to offload large, core, complex, and high-revenue-generating projects to the Center, to significantly increase its contributions to the company.

Chapter 7

Look Beyond Offshoring Only Peripheral Projects

A number of global companies are of the opinion that Offshore Center teams cannot execute core and complex projects. Hence, their tendency is to offload only simple projects to Offshore Centers, such as adding simple features to products, maintenance of legacy products, etc. The Offshore Center is then adding a large number of employees to the company but is not working on the company's core products/projects, which might have added increased revenues to the company compared to the Center's low revenue because of the simple projects.

Further, since the Offshore Center does not offer opportunities to work on challenging projects, it is unable to hire, retain, and motivate good talent, especially capable and experienced professionals. The Offshore Center teams then consist of inexperienced and mediocre professionals, who may even fail to deliver on the simple projects they receive. The HO does not offshore large projects then, fearing that they may not be successful because of the weak Offshore Center team. Thus, the team size and productivity of the Offshore Center remains low, resulting in low cost savings for the company.

This chapter argues that the assumption of head office (HO) management that Offshore Centers lack capable professionals is not correct. Countries where Offshore Centers are typically based have highly capable and experienced technical and management professionals, who can deliver on large and complex projects. The chapter suggests that companies capitalize on their Offshore Center talent by offering them large, complex, and high-revenue-generating projects that can add significantly to the company's revenues and provide increased cost savings during execution.

The chapter starts by describing the usual concerns of HO management about the lack of capabilities of their Offshore Center teams, which prevents the company from offshoring large and complex projects. It discusses the issues faced by the Offshore Center if it is given only peripheral projects, in terms of negative impact on the Offshore Center's contributions to the company's revenues and cost savings. The chapter then shows that the concerns of HO management about lack of good talent in the country of the Offshore Center are just plain myths. It highlights some facts to show that highly capable and experienced professionals work in countries where Offshore Centers are typically based, to show that these myths are not true. The chapter concludes by discussing how companies can capitalize on their highly capable Offshore Center talent by offering them high-value, large, and complex projects, which can significantly increase the contributions of the Offshore Center to the company's revenues and profits.

7.1. Concerns of Head Office Management

Head office management often does not offload high-end core development projects to Offshore Centers because they believe that the offshore teams do not have the requisite expertise and experience to execute such complex projects. As discussed in Chapter 2, the Offshore Center is generally located in a country of lesser economic status, while the HO is located in a country of high economic status. HO management often believes that because of the large salary difference between the country of the HO and the country of the Offshore Center, capable professionals in the country of the Offshore Center would have relocated to enhance their careers in the country of the HO (or to some other country with similar high economic status). Hence, HO management assumes that the professionals joining their Offshore Center are of mediocre capabilities and cannot be entrusted with execution of core and complex projects.

Further, a number of companies running Offshore Centers are product development companies. The HO management of these companies believes professionals in the countries of Offshore Centers have traditionally been executing service projects, having been working in the large number of services companies present in these countries. The HO management assumes that such professionals lack the aptitude, knowledge, capabilities, and skills required for developing products, since that is quite different from executing services projects. Thus, HO management does not offload core new product development projects to their Offshore Centers, fearing that these projects may not succeed. Instead, simple and peripheral projects, such as maintenance of legacy products, are offloaded, which the HO management believes can be executed by professionals without in-depth knowledge and expertise in product development.

7.2. Problems in Offshoring Only Peripheral Projects

The above approach of the HO management of offshoring only some peripheral projects creates a number of problems in the Offshore Center.

1. The teams in the Offshore Center are capable of delivering on more complex and challenging assignments. Since they are being offloaded only simple and low-revenue-generating projects, the Offshore Center's contributions to company revenues are quite limited. The Offshore Center then keeps growing in terms of adding more employees, but it fails to add significant value to the company. The full potential of the Offshore Center teams is not realized.

2. Since the employees in the Offshore Center are working on low-level tasks/projects, much below their capabilities, they become demotivated. Their job expectations are not being met because of the lack of challenges and opportunities in their jobs. They become demoralized, which is reflected in lower productivity and results in a severe negative impact on the deliverables of the Offshore Center. Such demoralization even causes attrition of experienced, senior, and capable Offshore Center employees, who decide to join companies that give them opportunities to work on more challenging projects.

    Thus, the Offshore Center has severe problems in motivating and retaining its core employees.

3. Experienced and capable technology professionals in the industry prefer to join companies that offer them opportunities to develop core products and work on complex, challenging, and exciting projects. Since the company's Offshore Center does not offer such opportunities, such professionals refuse to join it.

    Further, it becomes even more difficult to attract experienced managers from the industry, since they are managing large and highly complex projects in their current jobs. These senior managers refuse to join an Offshore Center where they would only have opportunities to manage some small and peripheral projects.

    Hence, the Offshore Center can recruit only mediocre performers with low experience levels, in both the technical and managerial ladders. The presence of such a weak team in the Offshore Center results in low productivity and output of the center. Thus, the cost-saving benefit for the company of offshoring becomes quite low.

Any company must realize that if its Offshore Center is expected to make any significant contributions, then it must have capable and experienced managers and technical professionals.

4. The basic purpose of the decision of the HO management to offshore only peripheral projects was that these projects would be successfully executed by what they assumed to be "mediocre professionals" in the Offshore Center. The irony is that with all the factors discussed above, even such peripheral projects start failing in the Offshore Center!

Let us consider the example of an Offshore Center being offloaded only projects to maintain large legacy products of the company. Since capable and experienced technical professionals and managers refuse to join the Offshore Center, their team consists only of mediocre professionals with limited experience. The HO management expects this team to deliver on the supposedly simple maintenance projects. However, the HO management fails to realize that even maintenance projects can have some complex requirements, which the inexperienced and mediocre talent in the Offshore Center will fail to handle.

- Customers keep demanding additional features in legacy products. Some of these features can be complex and can be implemented only by using new, advanced, and complex technologies. Since the Offshore Center team lacks professionals with expertise and experience in advanced technologies, the team fails to deliver on these tasks.

- The project teams are supposed to fix bugs (defects) being reported in the legacy products. Customers keep changing the environment of deployment of the products and that can sometimes result in exposing some complex defects in the products. If such defects are reported, then the project team needs to have capable and experienced technical professionals who can understand the complete architecture of the product to make modifications to resolve the bugs effectively, without impacting the functionality of the other features of the product. Unfortunately, the Offshore Center team will not have such experts among them and may fail to solve such bugs effectively, much to the displeasure of the customers.

- The management efforts required to manage a maintenance project effectively are no less than the efforts required to manage a development project. The project manager of a maintenance project needs to understand the new features requirements of multiple customers, collapse similar requirements of multiple customers into singular features, evaluate the impact of each of these features in consultation with the product management, select the set of features to be implemented, and manage the teams to implement these features within the customer-defined schedules. Further, the manager is continuously firefighting multiple critical bugs in the existing features of the product as they are reported by key customers. He or she not only needs to manage resolving these bugs within very tight deadlines but also needs to use his or her strong negotiation skills to keep the customer's concerns under control until the solutions are delivered.

These complex project management tasks can be fulfilled only by an experienced and capable project manager. However, since the Offshore Center fails to attract or retain such managers, its projects cannot be managed effectively. Thus, the team fails to deliver even on supposedly simple tasks of fixing defects and adding features to legacy products.

7.3. Eliminating the Myths of Head Office Management

All the above discussion shows that it is a poor idea for companies to offload only peripheral projects to their Offshore Centers. Companies are failing to realize the full potential of their Offshore Centers, purely because their HO management makes the assumption that Offshore Centers lack good talent.

This chapter will now show that the assumptions made by the HO management of lack of capable and experienced technical and management professionals in the countries where Offshore Centers are based are far from the truth. Countries where most Offshore Centers are located have quite good talent, who are at par with their counterparts in the HO of their parent companies. These Offshore Center professionals need only familiarity, mentoring, and training on the company's technologies and products to be able to handle core and complex projects successfully, similar to their HO counterparts.

Some of the myths believed by HO management, as discussed in Section 7.1, can now be disproved.

1. HO management assumes that since the countries of Offshore Centers have lower economic status, most of its capable and experienced professionals will have migrated to countries of higher economic status to gain better financial status and quality of life. However, this assumption is not correct. Typically, the Offshore Centers of global companies offer much higher compensation and perks to their employees compared to local companies in the countries of Offshore Centers. Thus, Offshore Center professionals have high economic status and lead comfortable lives compared to their peers in the industry in their country.

   Since the professionals in the countries of Offshore Centers have high status and sound financials despite remaining in their own countries, a large number of them stay in their own countries, *by choice*, rather than migrate to the countries of HOs of global companies. Thus, countries of Offshore Centers have excellent talent who can deliver on core and highly complex projects of global companies.

Further, professionals in the countries of the Offshore Centers think it is more prestigious to join a global company's Offshore Center than to join a local company because of the financial benefits and the opportunities to work with companies delivering global leading products and services. It is also a fact that professionals working in Offshore Centers of global leading companies are highly respected in their society in their countries.

Thus, Offshore Centers not only have access to excellent talent in their countries, they are also able to attract *the best* among this excellent talent. The assumption of HO management that the Offshore Center will not be able to deliver on core products/projects because it has less capable talent than the HO is not correct.

2. Another assumption of some global product development companies is that professionals in the countries of the Offshore Centers lack experience and expertise in developing products, since their experience has mostly been in the services industry. Such an argument might have been valid many years ago, but it is no longer valid now. Global leading product companies have been running Offshore Development Centers for many years, where they have trained a large number of professionals in these countries on product development techniques. These professionals now have extensive experience delivering on high-end products, and hence, any assumptions of their being able to execute only services projects are totally ill-founded.

Further, a large number of global venture capital (VC) companies, who were earlier based in countries such as the United States or Canada, or in Western Europe, now have vast presence in typical countries where Offshore Centers are based—such as India, Israel, and China. These VC companies have funded a number of successful local product start-ups in these countries in recent years. These local start-ups have developed global leading products totally from within their own countries. Thus, these local product start-ups now have a huge pool of talented professionals, whom the Offshore Centers of global product companies can tap.

Thus, global product companies have access to a large base of talented professionals in the countries of their Offshore Centers, both from existing Offshore Centers of other global product companies and from local VC-funded product start-ups, whom they can hire to deliver successfully on their core and complex products from within their Offshore Centers.

7.4. Benefits from Offshoring a Balanced Mix of Projects

Offshore Center management should share the above facts with HO management to refute their myths about there being a lack of excellent talent in their country. The Offshore Center management should share the following information to convince HO management to offshore core and complex projects to their teams.

1. The Offshore Center management should share the profiles of their key and senior technical and management employees with the HO management, highlighting their expertise and vast experience in handling large, core, and complex projects. They should not only showcase the existing talent in the Offshore Center but should also highlight the expertise of excellent talent available in the industry in their country, who can be attracted to join the Offshore Center in the near future, if they are given opportunities to work on core and complex projects. The HO management will then gain confidence that the Offshore Center teams have the strengths and experience to execute complex projects, and will agree to offshore such projects to them.

2. The Offshore Center management should work closely with the HO management to get *advance information* on upcoming core projects of the company and should then prepare their teams for winning such projects. For example, in the case of a product development company, the Offshore Center managers should work closely with the HO product management to get advance information on new key products being planned and should develop as much information as possible about the core features of these products. The Offshore Center managers should then train and groom their teams extensively in the business domains of these products and in the technologies to be used for implementing the core features of these products.

   Then, when the HO management decides to distribute the project tasks of developing such a new product among the HO and the Offshore Center, the Offshore Center managers can bid for implementing the core features of the product by highlighting the expertise developed by their teams in the business and technology domains of the product. The HO management can then compare the strengths of the Offshore Center team and the HO team in implementing various core features of the project and will decide to offload implementation of these features to the team with better strengths to deliver them successfully. Since the Offshore Center team will have developed expertise in implementing core features of the product, implementation of a large number of these core features will be offloaded to the Offshore Center for execution. Thus, the Offshore Center management will be able to win core and complex projects for their teams.

Thus, the Offshore Center teams will always have a mix of core projects and some peripheral projects, similar to the HO teams.

The opportunities to work on core and complex projects will help motivate and retain capable and senior Offshore Center employees. Further, the Offshore Center can attract highly capable and experienced technical professionals from the industry by highlighting the challenges being offered on its core and technologically advanced projects. Similarly, highly experienced managers from the industry will also join the Offshore Center, since they will get opportunities to manage large, core, and complex projects.

The Offshore Center can then build strong teams around these capable and senior professionals and deliver on complex and large projects. Since the Offshore Center teams will now be working on core and high-revenue-generating projects of the company, they will add significantly to the revenues and profits of the company.

Further, the presence of these experienced and strong professionals will also help the Offshore Center to deliver on its peripheral projects by overcoming the challenges mentioned in Section 7.2.

Section 7.2 discussed an example of an Offshore Center team working on a legacy product maintenance project that was unable to solve critical bugs or implement additional complex features in the product. The reasons for these failures were that the Offshore Center could not hire or retain capable and experienced technical professionals who could understand the complete product architecture and apply their knowledge of new and advanced technologies to deliver on these tasks.

Since the Offshore Center will now also be running complex new product development projects, it will be able to attract and retain experienced and capable technical professionals to work on such core projects. When inexperienced team members working on the maintenance project need help on the more complex tasks in their project, they can easily get it from these highly capable core technical professionals. Since these core technical professionals have extensive expertise in advanced technologies, they can easily help the maintenance project team find solutions to their problems. Thus, the Offshore Center will be able to deliver successfully on the maintenance projects tasks of resolving critical bugs and adding technologically advanced additional features to the product.

Further, Section 7.2 discussed the problems faced in successfully managing maintenance projects caused by the absence of experienced and capable managers in the Offshore Center. Again, since the Offshore Center will now have highly experienced and strong managers for managing core and complex new product development projects, these experienced managers can help and guide the managers of the maintenance projects in meeting their project management objectives. The managers of maintenance projects will then get the requisite support to allow them to manage their teams for successful implementation of additional features in the legacy products and for resolving customer-reported critical bugs within tight schedules to the satisfaction of the customers.

Thus, the full potential of Offshore Center teams will be realized, and they will be able to deliver successfully on all their projects, ranging from core and complex product development projects to maintenance projects.

* * * * *

Companies establish Offshore Centers to lower their costs for executing projects. However, the HO management in some companies over-insists on this cost reduction by severely limiting the necessary investments required in the Offshore Center—such as the investment required in offering attractive compensation for hiring and retaining excellent talent; the investment required in training and skill building of employees; and the investment required in acquiring requisite high-end hardware and software resources for execution of large, core, complex, and advanced technology projects. Chapter 8 will show that these constraints result in weakening of the Offshore Center delivery capability, and significantly limiting its contributions to the revenues and cost savings of the company. The chapter will present techniques for the Offshore Center management to convince the HO management to allow additional expenses for building the capacity of their teams, by presenting these expenses as necessary investments that will result in long-term cost savings and significant additions to the company's revenues from the Offshore Center. These long-term cost savings will far exceed, *by multiple factors*, these immediate high expenses incurred by the Offshore Center.

Chapter 8

Avoid Over-Insistence on the Cost-Reduction Purpose of the Offshore Center

The core reason for running an Offshore Center is to lower company costs, by offshoring projects to the low-cost location of the Offshore Center. However, some companies make all their decisions for the Offshore Center driven only by the cost-reduction factor. Over-insistence on cost reduction creates a number of constraints for the Offshore Center, such as in hiring and retaining excellent talent, reducing investments in training and skill building of employees, and lacking the requisite hardware and software resources for project execution. All these constraints lead to overall weakening of the Offshore Center delivery capability. Thus, Offshore Center output is reduced, resulting in an overall loss in the revenues and profits of the company.

This chapter suggests that companies should strike a fine balance between the cost reduction expected from the Offshore Center and the need to invest in strengthening the Offshore Center teams to maximize their contributions to the companies' revenues and profits. Companies should never try to reduce costs at the expense of compromising the delivery capabilities of the Offshore Center. The Offshore Center management should be given the flexibility to exceed the mandatory constraints on the cost savings expected from the Offshore Center to make higher investments in capacity building its staff. Such investments result in much higher revenue generation and cost savings from the Offshore Center in the long run.

The chapter starts by discussing the negative impact on Offshore Center delivery capabilities that result from over-insistence on the cost-reduction factor. It then suggests that companies offer flexibility to the Offshore Center management to make investments beyond their limited allocated budget, to strengthen the Offshore Center capabilities for achieving much higher cost savings for the company in the long run.

8.1. Weakening the Offshore Center's Delivery Capabilities by Over-Insistence on Cost Reduction

Companies expect significant savings in their costs of running projects in their Offshore Centers compared to running these projects in the head office (HO). The top management of the company expects the overall budget of the Offshore Center not to exceed a predefined maximum, to maintain a large differential between the cost of running the HO and the cost of running the Offshore Center.

Thus, hard upper bounds are set for the overall budget of the Offshore Center, which percolates down to setting hard bounds on various component budgets of the Offshore Center. Some of these component budgets include budgets for employee salaries, for training and building skills of employees, and for hardware and software resources required in the Offshore Center.

The Offshore Center management is then forced to make decisions in running the Offshore Center based on these budget constraints. Effectively, the decisions of the Offshore Center are driven *primarily* by the cost-reduction factor. This over-insistence on the cost-reduction factor weakens the Offshore Center for several reasons.

1. The Offshore Center puts a cap on the maximum possible salary to be given to employees at each level of the organization hierarchy, both in the technical ladder and in the management ladder, to prevent exceeding its overall salary budget. It is a known fact that highly capable professionals in the industry expect much more salary to change jobs compared to the usual industry norms of salary at their levels. Since the Offshore Center management is not given the flexibility to relax the salary norms to attract such professionals, the Offshore Center fails to hire highly capable professionals from the industry, as it cannot match their salary expectations.

   These excellent professionals might have significantly strengthened the delivery capabilities of the Offshore Center. For example, the presence of a highly capable technical expert might have allowed the Offshore Center to design and implement large and complex projects. Thus, the ability of the Offshore Center to take core projects and its delivery capabilities on such projects might have been significantly strengthened. Unfortunately, the Offshore Center misses such opportunities because it is unable to hire such professionals (refer to Case Study 8.1 at the end of the chapter).

2. The Offshore Center may already have some highly capable employees. However, since the Offshore Center has defined upper limits on their maximum possible salaries, these professionals will receive smaller annual salary increases than some of their peers with similar capabilities in the industry. These employees will feel frustrated and, in the long term, may decide to quit the Offshore Center to join a company willing to pay them higher salaries. Thus, the Offshore Center will see attrition of its capable employees, resulting in weakening its delivery capabilities.

3. Offshore Center professionals need to continuously upgrade their knowledge to improve their productivity and contributions to the company. They need to learn new techniques that help them speed up the execution of their projects, improve the quality of the project deliverables, and achieve higher customer satisfaction. For example, employees in a software development company who are using the traditional project execution methodologies may need to learn new and improved methodologies, such as the iterative Agile methodology, to improve their project deliverables.

   Thus, the Offshore Center needs to invest in building the skills of its employees by regularly training them on new techniques, methodologies, and processes. The investments in acquiring such training for the employees can be large. If the training budget of the Offshore Center is seriously constrained, it can either not conduct sufficient training or include only a small number of employees in the training classes. The Offshore Center then fails to enhance the skills of most of its employees. Overall employee productivity remains low, the speed of project execution remains slow, and the quality of project deliverables suffers. The contributions of the Offshore Center to the success of the company's projects are severely constrained.

4. The last chapter suggested that the Offshore Center management seek advance information on upcoming high-revenue-generating projects of the company and train its employees extensively in the advanced technologies to be used in these projects. The Offshore Center teams can then bid for, and obtain, these new projects (instead of receiving only peripheral projects), which may significantly enhance their contributions to the company's revenues.

   However, most new and advanced technologies require advanced hardware and expensive software tools for their implementation. If employees need to learn these advanced technologies, then the Offshore Center must be willing to make large investments in its hardware and software resources.

Unfortunately, since the budgets for resources in the Offshore Center are low, it fails to make investments in purchasing the needed hardware and software resources. The Offshore Center employees then cannot learn complex and advanced technologies, and the HO management will not offload complex projects to the Center; it will continue to offload only low-revenue-generating peripheral projects to the Center. The contributions of the Offshore Center to company's revenues and profits remain low.

In comparison, the HO is allocated much higher budgets compared to the Offshore Center. It can invest heavily in hardware and software resources required to train its employees in the advanced technologies being used in the company's complex projects. The complex projects remain in the HO, since its employees have the knowledge and expertise in the technologies needed for these projects.

All the above factors result in overall weakening of the delivery capabilities of the Offshore Center teams. A weak Offshore Center imposes restrictions on the size and type of projects the HO can offload to the Offshore Center, since there are fears that large and complex projects may not succeed. Hence, large and complex projects still end up being executed within the HO, leading to the HO team remaining large, and the Offshore Center team remaining small.

The irony is that the steps being taken by the company to lower its costs, by constraining the budgets of the Offshore Center, end up forcing the company to *increase its costs significantly*, by hiring more people in the HO instead of the Offshore Center!

8.2. Invest in Strengthening Offshore Center Capabilities for Long-Term Cost Savings

Companies must realize that their insistence on imposing hard constraints on the budgets of the Offshore Centers limits severely the ability of the Offshore Center management to invest in building and strengthening their teams. If an Offshore Center is to make any useful contribution to the parent company, it must have strong teams. The company should avoid reducing its costs at the expense of compromising the delivery capabilities of the Offshore Center.

Since the main purpose of running an Offshore Center is to reduce the costs of the company, the company should go through the usual exercise of deciding the upper bounds on the budget of the Offshore Center that can give the company requisite cost savings. However, these bounds on the budget must not be hard rules to be followed by the Offshore Center management; they should, rather, be *broad guidelines* to be followed. The Offshore Center management should be given flexibility to exceed these budgets if additional expenses, and the business case is made for these expenses, are required to strengthen the Center's capabilities in hiring, retaining, and training talent.

The Offshore Center management should convince the HO management of the value of exceeding its allocated expenses by presenting these additional expenses as *necessary investments* that will result in long-term cost savings and significant additions to the company's revenues from the Offshore Center. If the Offshore Center management can project that these long-term cost savings will far exceed the immediate high expenses being incurred by the Offshore Center, then the HO management may decide to approve these expenses as long-term investments.

For example, the previous section discussed the case of an Offshore Center not being able to hire an excellent technical expert because of salary expectations that far exceed the Offshore Center's norm for salary at this level. If the Offshore Center management approaches the HO management seeking their approval for such a high salary for a candidate to be hired, their request will be deemed unreasonable and will invariably be rejected. The Offshore Center management should instead follow a different approach to convince the HO management.

Let us assume that the company is developing products for which the projects for developing these products are distributed among the engineering teams in the HO and the Offshore Center. The Offshore Center management should share with the HO management that the Center lacks a capable technical expert who can play the role of a strong "technical architect." Without such a capable technical architect, the Offshore Center cannot design new and complex products or their intricate features. Thus, the Offshore Center can be given only peripheral projects to perform, such as development of simple low-end products or addition of nonsignificant features to the core products. Since these projects are not complex and are low-revenue-generating projects for the company, the contributions of the Offshore Center to the revenues of the company are limited. Further, these simple projects require only small implementation teams, which results in the overall team size of the Offshore Center remaining small. Thus, the cost saving for the company from offshoring is also low.

The Offshore Center management should instead share a detailed proposal with the HO management of the long-term benefits to be achieved by hiring such a technical expert. The Offshore Center management should explain that a strong technical architect can design and facilitate development of new and complex products for the company from wholly within the Offshore Center.

The Offshore Center should also be able to recruit and build strong technical teams around this technical expert. He or she can effectively train and guide these technical personnel for them to take up the tasks of designing and implementing new and complex features of the company's products.

Thus, the company can then offload complex projects of development of its new and complex products to the Offshore Center. The projects will be larger, to capitalize on the availability of a large number of trained technical experts in the Offshore Center. The Offshore Center will then be executing high-revenue-generating projects for the company and will significantly increase its team size to deliver on these large projects. The contributions of the Offshore Center to the revenues and cost savings of the company will then be quite high.

Such projections from the Offshore Center management can convince the HO management that the long-term revenue increase and cost savings with this technical expert will exceed, *by multiple factors,* the current expenses of his or her higher compensation. The HO management will then perceive the request for the high salary for the candidate purely as a long-term investment for the company and may approve hiring this expert.

Similarly, the Offshore Center management should be given flexibility in investing in training and skill building of its teams. The teams can then be trained on improved project delivery techniques and methodologies to achieve multiple benefits.

- The productivity of the Offshore Center teams will improve, leading to the Center making higher contributions to the revenues of the company.
- The project delivery time will be shortened, leading to lower costs of project execution in the Offshore Center.
- The quality of project deliverables will improve, leading to higher customer satisfaction for projects executed from the Offshore Center.

Finally, companies are aware that the prices of most of the high-end hardware and software tools from global vendors are similar across the globe, regardless of the economic status of the country where they are purchased. Hence, the cost of purchasing such equipment and tools will be similar in the country of the HO and the country of the Offshore Center. Companies should decouple the budget allocation for the cost of acquisition of such hardware and software resources from the rest of the Offshore Center budget, which can be expected to be much lower than the HO budget. Instead, companies should create a separate budget for such resource acquisition for their *global engineering division as a whole,* including both the HO and the Offshore Center engineering teams.

Investment in these resources will then not be constrained by the Offshore Center's low budget. The same norms will be followed for acquiring these resources in the HO and the Offshore Center, and both will be able to purchase the resources required by their teams. The Offshore Center can then acquire the requisite high-end hardware and software resources to train its employees in advanced technologies to be used in the core projects of the company. The Offshore Center teams can then receive these core and complex projects, which will significantly enhance their contributions to the company's revenues.

Case Study 8.1

A global software product development company was running an Offshore Center. The company had prescribed strict upper bounds for employee salaries in the Offshore Center at each level of the organization hierarchy, to achieve higher cost savings with offshoring. The maximum salary for an Offshore Center employee at each level in the organization hierarchy was capped at only a fraction of the salary of an HO employee at the same level.

The company was developing high-end products based on advanced technologies. Thus, the work was quite interesting and challenging for technology professionals. A number of experienced and capable candidates from the industry applied for jobs in the Offshore Center of the company.

The Institute of Electrical and Electronics Engineers (IEEE) is the largest body of engineers in the world in the electrical, electronics, computers, and communications domains. The highest technical grade in IEEE is the "Fellow" grade. The body follows strict selection norms to promote its highly distinguished members with excellent achievements in their technical domains to the Fellow grade. Only 0.1% of IEEE members worldwide are promoted to the Fellow grade.

The company, so far, had no IEEE Fellow as an employee, not even in the HO. An IEEE Fellow in the country of the Offshore Center applied for the technical architect position in the Offshore Center. He was a globally recognized expert in the technology domain of the products of the company. Thus, he had the ability to add significant value to the company with his proven expertise and experience.

Needless to say, the Offshore Center decided to hire him for the position. He was expecting a salary package commensurate with his capabilities. However, as per the company policy, the Offshore Center architect could only be paid a fraction of the maximum salary drawn by his counterpart HO architects.

Unfortunately, the salary expectation of the candidate was much beyond this salary cap. The Offshore Center decided to reject his salary demand and failed to hire him. Interestingly, the candidate was much more capable than his counterpart architects in the HO, with whom his salary was being compared!

Thus, the Offshore Center lost an excellent candidate because of the rigid attitude of the company. It was, indeed, a major loss to the Offshore Center, since he could have contributed to developing technologically advanced, complex, and high-revenue-generating products from within the Offshore Center, which would have significantly increased the contributions of the Center to the company.

This candidate instead joined a purely local company, which agreed to match his salary expectations. That local company was not constrained to keep his salary at a fraction of any HO architects in a different country, since the company had no Engineering Center in any other country!

Thus, the Offshore Center was at a disadvantageous position even compared to the local companies in its country, where the local management was given full authority to make employee hiring decisions.

Solution

Companies must realize that it is quite difficult to find talented candidates. If such a candidate is found, he or she must be offered a position immediately, giving the candidate a reasonable increase over his or her current salary as based on expectations. Companies should not get entangled in rigid salary range norms for such a candidate.

The Offshore Center so far had technical teams with only mediocre talent. Hence, the Center was executing only small and peripheral projects for the company. These projects were generating low revenues, and the cost savings were also low. Thus, the overall value added by the Offshore Center to the global company was low.

As mentioned in the previous section, the Offshore Center management should have highlighted to the HO management that such an architect could use his expertise in advanced technologies to design large and core products of the company from entirely within the Offshore Center. The Offshore Center would have also been able to build large and strong technical teams around him, to execute large projects. Thus, the Offshore Center would have been able to execute large high-revenue-generating projects with much higher cost savings compared to executing just small peripheral projects. Thus, the HO management could be convinced to hire this candidate, since the differential cost in paying a high salary to the candidate would become insignificant in the long run, compared to high revenue additions and cost savings from his presence.

* * * * *

Offshore Centers recognize the contributions of their high-performing employees by instituting a number of awards, such as the "Employee of the Month" award, "Team of the Month" award, "Peer Appreciation" award, etc. The purpose of such awards is to motivate the employees to perform beyond their potential to achieve such recognitions, resulting in an increase in their productivity. Since these awards are instituted *locally* within the Offshore Center, employees compete only with their peer employees in the Center. Such competition may not be hard enough to force the employees to significantly improve their performance to win the awards. Since a number of projects within the Offshore Center are extensions to the core projects being executed in the HO, employees in both locations are working on similar tasks. Chapter 9 will suggest that companies capitalize on this fact and institute *global* awards, where all the employees of the Offshore Center and the HO can contend to win awards. The Offshore Center employees will then also need to compete with high performers from the HO, who are working on the company's core and complex projects. The Offshore Center employees will then have to stretch themselves much beyond their potential to win these awards, resulting in much greater improvement in their productivity compared to the small improvement gained from local awards.

Chapter 9

Unified Awards across the Offshore Center and the Head Office

Offshore Centers recognize and award the contributions of their high-performing employees in multiple fashions. One usual method is instituting an "Employee of the Month" award (and other similar awards) in the Offshore Center. The performance and contributions of all the employees in that month are evaluated by a selection committee consisting of Offshore Center managers. The committee uses strict selection criteria to select the employee making the most critical contributions as the "Employee of the Month." The employee is then publically recognized and awarded for his or her performance.

The purpose of instituting such awards is to reward high performers for their contributions and to motivate the rest of the employees to perform beyond their potential to achieve such recognition. Thus, the Offshore Center employees work toward improving their performance to win the awards. The productivity of the Offshore Center employees rises, resulting in the Center making much higher contributions to the parent company.

Such awards are usually instituted *locally* within the Offshore Center. Since the employees compete only with their peer Offshore Center employees, the competition to win the awards may not be very hard for high-performing employees. Such a competition does not force such employees to significantly improve their performance to win the awards. The overall improvement in the performance and productivity of the Offshore Center employees remains low.

It is a known fact that a large number of projects within the Offshore Center are extensions to the core projects being executed in the HO. The Offshore Center teams working on their project modules also have counterpart teams in the HO working on other modules of the same projects. Thus, employees in both locations are working on similar tasks, are working toward meeting similar project objectives, are evaluated on similar performance parameters, etc. This chapter suggests that Offshore Centers capitalize on this fact to maximize the benefits from their awards.

The chapter suggests that instead of having a local award, the Offshore Center management work with the head office (HO) management to institute a *global* "Employee of the Month" award. The award should consider the HO and Offshore Center as a single cohesive unit. All the employees of the HO and Offshore Center should be in contention for the award, which should be decided by a selection committee consisting of HO and Offshore Center management.

Such a global award will mean that Offshore Center employees compete directly with HO employees. The HO will usually have a number of high performers who are working on core and complex projects of the company. Thus, the high performers of the Offshore Center not only have to compete with a larger population of employees, they are now up against many high performers who are excelling on core projects. The Offshore Center employees will then have to stretch themselves much beyond their potential to be able to compete successfully with such excellent talent and win the awards. The Offshore Center employees will then keep raising their performance levels, leading to much higher improvement in the overall productivity and performance of the Offshore Center compared to the small improvement gained from the local awards.

This chapter starts by discussing the limitations of having purely local awards in the Offshore Center. It then suggests that Offshore Center management instead institute global awards, including both Offshore Center and HO employees, and elaborates the benefits of this approach. The chapter also discusses the method for running such global awards in large companies having multiple divisions. In some companies, there is still a huge gap between the complexity of the projects being executed in the HO and in the Offshore Center. Since the complexity and quality of the projects being offloaded to the Offshore Center may not be at the same level as the HO projects, it may be difficult for Offshore Center employees to showcase their full potential and compete with their HO counterparts to win these global awards. The chapter suggests solutions to this problem by describing the need to create fair evaluation criteria for global awards that give equal opportunity to all the employees to win the awards, regardless of the type, category, and complexity of their projects. It then discusses the unfortunate scenario where the Offshore Center employees repeatedly fail to win these global awards, and there is almost a total domination of

HO employees in winning the awards. It analyzes the possible reasons for this result and suggests steps to be taken by the Offshore Center management to rectify the problems. The chapter concludes by recommending against creating quotas for Offshore Center employees in the global awards to address the issue of them not winning the awards. It argues that such a solution will defeat the basic purpose of instituting global awards.

9.1. Limitations of Local Awards within the Offshore Center

Offshore Centers generally institute a number of awards to recognize the performance and contributions of their employees. Some of these awards may include an "Employee of the Month" award to recognize the best-performing employee for that month, a "Team of the Month" award to recognize high-performing project teams, a "Peer Appreciation" award for employees to recognize the efforts and help of their peer employees, etc. The desire to win such recognition motivates employees to put additional effort into their work to improve their performance. As the performance of the employees improves, the result is higher overall productivity of the Offshore Center.

This chapter focuses mostly on the "Employee of the Month" award. The approaches described in the chapter can be applied to the other awards as well, and the text will refer specifically to these other awards wherever required.

These awards are local to the Offshore Center. A selection committee consisting of managers in the Offshore Center evaluates the contributions of all the Offshore Center employees and selects the employee making the maximum contribution as the awardee. However, such an approach of running purely local awards in the Offshore Center has limitations.

1. Employees are competing only locally with their peer employees in the Offshore Center. Thus, the competition is limited and high performers do not need to strive to work beyond their potential to win the awards.

2. In some companies, the HO management is mostly offloading peripheral projects to the Offshore Centers along with a few core projects. The Offshore Center employees working on the peripheral projects have limited challenges, which prevent them from showcasing their full potential. Hence, a large base of Offshore Center employees is rarely in contention for these awards. The very small set of employees working on the core and complex projects in the Offshore Center then becomes eligible for these awards by displaying a small improvement in their performance, since these employees face limited competition. Thus, the overall performance

improvement gained from these local awards is not significant, defeating the very purpose of instituting these awards.

3. A large number of Offshore Center projects are extensions to the core projects being executed in the HO. The teams working on these projects in the Offshore Center are effectively a part of the overall global project teams, including the HO and Offshore Center. For the success of such multilocation projects, these teams in the Offshore Center and the HO must integrate and work cohesively as a unit.

   However, if separate employee awards are instituted locally in the HO and the Offshore Center, then both units remain separate silos. Employees in each location are competing with employees within their location only, even though the employees in the other location are also working on the same overall projects. Thus, instituting such local awards does not facilitate close integration of the teams in the HO and the Offshore Center, which could have resulted in better team cohesiveness and cooperation required for high success of overall project deliverables.

9.2. Benefits of Instituting Global Awards

As discussed, many projects of the Offshore Center and HO are closely interlinked. The teams in these separate locations are thus working on the same overall projects. The Offshore Centers should capitalize on this fact to extract more benefit from their awards.

Instead of having only local awards, the Offshore Center management and the HO management should work together to convert these awards to global awards. A single "Employee of the Month" award should be instituted for both locations, covering both the Offshore Center and the HO employees. The selection for the award should be made by a committee having fair representation of the Offshore Center and HO managers. The award decisions should be made by consensus in the committee to ensure fairness in the selection process.

Our suggested approach for instituting global awards will result in multiple benefits to the Offshore Center.

1. Offshore Center employees will now have to compete with HO employees in addition to competing with their peer employees in the Offshore Center. A larger base of competing employees will require the Offshore Center employees to put in additional effort to win the "Employee of the Month" award.

   Further, in some companies, most of the core projects are executed in the HO, while the Offshore Center mostly works on peripheral projects.

The Offshore Center employees will now have to compete with a large number of strong HO employees working on core and complex projects, instead of competing with a large number of their peer Offshore Center employees working on simple and peripheral projects. Since core projects offer immense opportunities for employees to showcase their full potential, these HO employees will make it difficult for the Offshore Center employees to attain an award. Thus, the Offshore Center employees will need to stretch beyond their limits of performance to be able to compete to win these awards. Offshore Center employees will then put in huge additional effort and significantly improve their performance. The overall productivity of the Offshore Center will then increase much more than when the employees were competing only for local awards.

Similarly, for the global "Team of the Month" award, the project teams within the Offshore Center will have to compete with strong project teams in the HO. The members of the Offshore Center project teams will then need to put in additional individual effort and work more closely with each other, as a strong cohesive unit, to demonstrate better team results than their HO counterpart teams. This will result in better bonding within the Offshore Center project teams, leading to higher success in their projects.

2. Since a large number of projects in the Offshore Center and HO are quite interlinked and have a number of interdependencies, these should ideally follow the same norms of project execution. It was suggested in Section 4.5 that the HO management implement the same practices for executing projects in the Offshore Center as are being followed in the HO, such as following the same project execution methodologies, project delivery processes, documentation standards, etc. Such mechanisms ensure close integration of project teams in the Offshore Center and HO, resulting in a higher degree of success of their closely interlinked projects.

The institution of global awards will further strengthen this integration of teams in the two locations. The employees in the Offshore Center will be competing with both their peer employees in the Offshore Center and with their peers in the HO to win these awards. The Offshore Center employees will learn more about the projects, activities, capabilities, and performance of their counterpart HO employees, in the same way as they are aware of these facts about their peer Offshore Center employees. The Offshore Center employees will then perceive all these employees as their peers, belonging to a single *global team* working on the same overall projects. Thus, the location boundaries will disappear, and the two locations will no longer be perceived as separate silos. Offshore Center and the HO teams will be working as a single cohesive team, which is ideal for successful delivery of their closely interlinked projects.

Similar close integration between locations can be achieved by making the "Peer Appreciation" award global. The award is recommended by an employee to recognize another peer employee who has provided tremendous help, support, mentoring, and training to him or her, by going beyond one's call of duty, to allow him or her to meet his or her project objectives. Since global awards consider employees in both locations as being part of a single unit, the Peer Appreciation award can be recommended by an HO employee for an Offshore Center employee who is working on the extension of the same project as the HO employee and has helped him or her on that project, and vice versa. Such award recommendations across the location boundaries will result in improved bonding, respect, and trust among the Offshore Center and HO employees. Thus, close integration between multilocation teams will be achieved, resulting in a higher success rate of the overall projects being executed by these teams.

It is interesting to discuss here a special case of the global "Team of the Month" award, which will result in very close integration between multilocation project teams working on a single overall project. Sometimes companies run small projects for which most of the team members are based in the HO and a very small number of members are based in the Offshore Center. Such a small team in the Offshore Center does not justify having a local project manager to manage the team, so the entire project team is directed by the HO project manager, who manages both the HO and the Offshore Center project team members. In such projects, the award selection committee can consider this multilocation team as a single "Project Team" to be considered for the team award. Thus, the project team members in the HO and the Offshore Center will work closely with each other and will help and support each other, to achieve higher success on their project so as to win the award. Such acts result in true integration of multilocation project teams, a highly desirable requirement for multilocation projects to succeed.

3. It was mentioned in Chapter 7 that some companies offload mostly peripheral projects to their Offshore Centers, and only a few core projects are offloaded. It was suggested that the Offshore Center management highlight the capabilities of their core employees to the HO management to convince them that the Offshore Center teams can execute large, core, and complex projects. The HO management may then be convinced to offshore such core projects.

The Offshore Center management can capitalize on the results of the global awards to further buttress their claims being put forward to the HO management on the strengths of their core employees in executing complex projects. The selection committee of the "Global Employee of the Month" award has senior HO managers as its members, along with senior Offshore Center managers. The selection committee evaluates the performance of the Offshore Center employees on various parameters in competition with the HO employees. If their selection process results in a large number of Offshore Center employees winning the global award, *month after month*, then these senior HO managers will realize that the Offshore Center has excellent talent, comparable to the talent available in the HO. The Offshore Center management should then use this fact to impress upon the HO management that the Offshore Center has the talent to execute core and complex projects. They should bring to the notice of the HO management that this excellent Offshore Center talent is heavily underutilized, since these employees are working on low-revenue-generating small and peripheral projects. The HO management may then be convinced that the Offshore Center has the requisite talent to execute even core and complex projects and may offload such projects to the Offshore Center. The Offshore Center can then make much higher contributions to the revenues of the company.

4. Chapter 5 discussed the need for senior and deserving Offshore Center employees to grow to the global top positions. The decision on promoting employees to global top positions is usually made by a selection committee consisting of the company's senior management. It was suggested that the committee should also include senior Offshore Center management personnel, who can then raise the case of their senior employees for promotions to global top levels.

   Institution of global awards can help the Offshore Center management to strengthen the cases of their senior employees in the selection committee deliberations. If a senior Offshore Center employee is repeatedly winning the "Global Employee of the Month" award against stiff competition from senior HO employees, then the Offshore Center management should use this fact to highlight the capabilities of the employee to the selection committee for global top positions. The selection committee will want to promote the best candidates globally from all the HO and Offshore Center employees to the global top positions. The selection committee will realize that the performance of this Offshore Center employee was evaluated using strict parameters by a group of senior HO and Offshore Center managers. The employee was deemed to be showing excellent results compared to senior HO employees if he or she received the award several times. The selection committee members will then appreciate the fact that this employee is a deserving candidate among all the other candidates (including HO candidates) being considered for promotion to global top positions. Thus, the candidature of this Offshore Center employee will be considered favorably by the selection committee when making a decision on promotions to global top positions.

9.3. Global Awards in Companies with Multiple Product Divisions

Chapter 6 described the organization structures of large product development companies that are developing multiple products. Such a company will have individual product divisions reporting to their respective vice presidents for engineering in the HO (see Figure 9-1). He or she has some engineering directors in the HO reporting to him or her, who in turn have some project managers

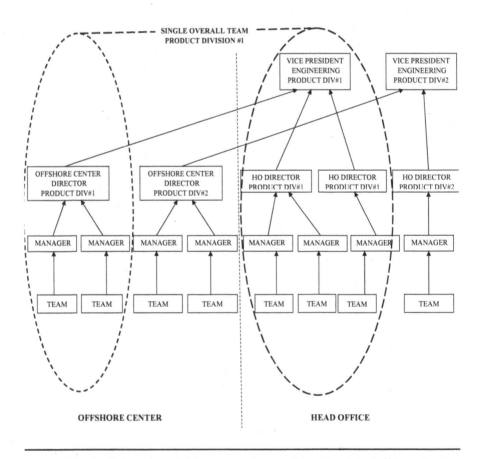

Figure 9-1   Global product divisions spread across the HO and the Offshore Center.

and their teams under them. Each of these product divisions has its extended teams in the Offshore Center.

The teams of each product division in the Offshore Center report to their project managers, who in turn report to their engineering directors in the Offshore Center. These Offshore Center engineering directors report to their respective product division vice presidents in the HO. Thus, effectively, each global product division vice president is handing a single overall team, which is spread across the HO and the Offshore Center (shown in Figure 9-1 as joined ellipses).

Such companies with independent product development divisions should institute individual "Global Employee of the Month" awards for each global product division instead of instituting a single award for the entire company. Each individual award should cover both the HO and Offshore Center employees *working in that product division*.

The following are reasons to have specific global awards for each product division instead of company-wide global awards.

1. Each global product division is working on a single product. The teams in the HO and Offshore Center of that product division are working on various project modules for developing that product. It is important for these project teams to integrate and work as a cohesive unit for success of the product. This purpose can be achieved by instituting a global award specific to this product division. Instituting a global award across multiple disparate product divisions will result only in integrating teams working on unrelated products/projects, which is not a requirement for success of these projects.

2. The HO and Offshore Center employees in a single product division are working on similar projects and technologies. Thus, their performance can be compared using the same set of parameters. The process of evaluating their performance for deciding the awardees will then be objective and fair, as opposed to comparing performances of employees in different product divisions, who are working on totally different sets of products, projects, and technologies. Thus, employees will gain confidence in the fairness of the award evaluation process if the global awards are specific to individual product divisions.

3. The selection committee for each product division global award will consist of the senior management team of that division, with representation from both the HO and the Offshore Center. For example, for Product Division #1 shown in Figure 9-1, the selection committee will consist of the product division vice president for engineering, the Offshore Center engineering director, and the HO engineering directors (all shown within the ellipses). Each of these selection committee members is well aware of

the overall product requirements and can understand the work and effort involved in various project modules being executed for developing the product. Thus, the Offshore Center engineering director will be aware of the work being done by the HO employees on their project modules despite his not being based in the HO. Similarly, the HO engineering directors will understand the work being done by the Offshore Center employees on their project modules. The members of the selection committee are then quite knowledgeable and can compare the performance of the employees across the locations, and will be able reach a good decision on the awardees. The process of award selection will then be entirely fair, despite the candidates working in different locations.

In contrast, if the global award is spread across multiple product divisions, then the selection committee members belonging to one product division will be only barely knowledgeable about the projects being executed in the other product divisions. They will not be able to evaluate and judge fairly the complexity of the work being performed by various candidates and the criticality of their contributions to the success of their products. The selection committee will thus not be able to compare the performance of the candidates objectively and may end up making subjective decisions. The employees may then perceive that less deserving candidates are winning awards, which will demotivate many high-performing employees.

Besides having the "Employee of the Month" within the product division, the project teams within the division itself should compete for the "Team of the Month" award, across locations. Further, the employees of the division should recommend their fellow employees within the division itself, across locations, for the "Peer Appreciation" award.

9.4. Fair Evaluation Criteria for Global Awards

As mentioned earlier, in some companies there is still a big gap between the complexities of the projects being executed in the HO and the projects being executed in the Offshore Center. The HO teams are mostly given core and complex projects, such as the design and development of core products of the company. In contrast, the Offshore Center is offloaded mostly simple and peripheral projects, such as maintenance of legacy products or addition of simple features to the products. The Offshore Center employees working on such peripheral projects thus have limited challenges and cannot showcase their full potential to compete for global awards with their HO counterparts, who are working on core projects.

A general tendency is that the managers on award selection committees assume that since design and implementation of core projects involves highly intricate and complex tasks, the employees working on such projects deserve to win awards as compared to employees working on supposedly simple peripheral projects. These selection committees then repeatedly confer the global awards on HO employees, since a large number of them are working on core projects, while the Offshore Center employees rarely win these awards.

The lack of global awards to Offshore Center employees leads to a sense of injustice and discrimination among them. They become demoralized and their performance and productivity suffer. Although the purpose of instituting global awards is to motivate the Offshore Center employees to improve their performance, it instead results in the totally opposite effect on the Offshore Center employees.

This issue should be addressed by defining a fair set of criteria for deciding the global awards. The criteria should recognize high performance in all types and categories of projects—from large, core, and complex projects to simple and peripheral projects.

The HO and Offshore Center managers on the selection committee should work together to define a set of unique parameters for each category of projects being executed in the company, such as core product development projects, maintenance projects, etc. The performance of the employees on their projects is then evaluated based on the results shown by them on the respective parameters of their category of projects. Employees who excel on the defined parameters for their category of projects can then be considered at par with employees who excel on the defined parameters for other categories of projects, regardless of the perceived complexity of the category of projects. Such an approach will ensure that all the employees have an equal opportunity to be selected as winners of global awards, without any bias for any project categories or complexities.

For example, some of the evaluation parameters for core product development projects might be the performance of the employee in creating an optimal architecture and design of the product, implementing features that have better speed/performance than similar features in competing products, producing high-quality product deliverables, meeting the product requirements to the satisfaction of the key customers, etc. If an employee shows excellent results on some of these parameters, then he or she is considered a deserving candidate for the global award.

In contrast, some of the evaluation parameters for maintenance projects of legacy products might be the ability of the employee to solve critical bugs reported by key customers that required deep understanding of the architecture and design of the product so as to make requisite modifications, very short turnaround time in solving critical bugs to the satisfaction of the customer, ability to add customer-required new and important features to the product, etc. If an employee shows excellent results on some of these parameters, then he or she can be considered a candidate for the global award in the same way as the above-described employee, who shows excellent results in core development projects.

Thus, the evaluation process for global awards selection will be fair, just, and objective. Deserving employees of both the Offshore Center and the HO will have equal opportunities to win these awards, regardless of their category and complexity of projects. The most capable Offshore Center employees, even on peripheral projects, would start winning the global awards. The employees in the Offshore Center would then perceive the award selection criteria to be fair to them and would start working on improving their performance to compete for these awards. The purpose of using global awards to motivate Offshore Center employees to improve their productivity would then be met successfully.

9.5. Proposed Actions if Offshore Center Employees Fail to Win Global Awards

It may be that, despite the company creating the above-described fair evaluation criteria for global awards, the Offshore Center employees may still not be winning these awards or may be winning them only occasionally. Instead, HO employees may be winning these awards almost on a regular basis. Such a situation should be a matter of concern for the Offshore Center management and should trigger serious thought and action among them.

The Offshore Center management should investigate the root causes for their employees not winning the awards and should offer the following solutions.

1. The Offshore Center managers and the HO managers on the global award selection committee should analyze the various categories of projects being offloaded to the Offshore Center. If the evaluation parameters of some of these project categories are strict compared to the evaluation parameters defined for other project categories, the selection committee members should refine the parameters to make them comparable. If employees are excelling on some aspects of project delivery in some project categories, but those aspects are not included in any of the evaluation parameters for that category, then additional evaluation parameters should be defined for that category. Thus, refining the evaluation parameters of the category of projects being executed in the Offshore Center will allow employees who excel in these project categories to win the global awards.

2. If, despite having well-defined evaluation parameters for all categories of projects, the Offshore Center employees are still not showing good results

on these parameters, then the management should seriously question the quality of projects being offloaded to the Offshore Center. It might be that even though well-defined evaluation parameters are available for the categories of projects being offloaded to the Offshore Center, the projects in those categories themselves are so mundane and weak that no Offshore Center employee has a real opportunity to excel on these parameters. In comparison, projects of higher complexity in these categories are given to the HO, allowing their employees to excel on their evaluation parameters.

Offshore Center management should then *convert this constraint to an opportunity* to win more complex and challenging projects from the HO. The Offshore Center management should highlight to the HO management that the projects being offloaded to their teams are of low value-add to the company, are of extremely low complexity, and are offering minimal challenges to the project teams. The Offshore Center teams have the skills and experience to excel on more core and complex projects that could allow the Offshore Center to make much higher contributions to the company's revenues. The HO management might then be convinced to offload more core and complex projects to the Offshore Center.

3. If the Offshore Center managers realize that their employees are not winning the awards because most of these employees do not have the right skills and experience for their projects, this should convince them to improve their employee hiring norms.

    The previous chapter noted that a key reason why the Offshore Center is unable to hire good talent is because of constraints on its salary budgets. It was suggested that the Offshore Center management should convince the HO management to relax the hard upper bounds on salaries to be able to hire excellent candidates. The fact that Offshore Center employees are not winning global awards can be used by the Offshore Center management as an additional data point to convince the HO management on this aspect. The Offshore Center management should share with the HO management that they were not able to hire candidates with the needed expertise who could have delivered excellent results to win these global awards, as they were unable to meet their salary expectations. The HO management might then be concerned that lack of good talent in the Offshore Center would hurt the project deliverables and would agree to relax the salary caps to allow the Offshore Center to hire capable candidates.

4. If the Offshore Center management realizes that their employees are not winning the awards because their employees do not have the right training on the project execution techniques and technologies being used in their projects, that should tell the Offshore Center management that they need to improve their employee training and skill-building practices.

The previous chapter mentioned that companies often provide limited funding in the training budgets for Offshore Center employees. The Offshore Center management should highlight to the HO management that their employees are not showing good results on their projects, to be able to win the global awards, because they lack the requisite training to deliver effectively on their projects. This argument might convince the HO management to increase the budget for training and skill building of the Offshore Center teams so that they will be able to perform at a similar level as their counterpart HO teams.

Similarly, the Offshore Center management should use the same argument with the HO management to request higher budgets for hardware and software resources required for the Offshore Center employees to learn advanced high-end technologies being used in core projects of the company.

The HO management will appreciate the fact that since both the HO and the Offshore Center teams are working on the same overall project, both teams must produce a similar high quality of deliverables for the success of the overall project, and may then allocate higher budgets for training and hardware/software resources for the Offshore Center teams.

9.6. Avoid Quotas in Global Awards

The problem of Offshore Center employees not winning global awards should be addressed only by following the above-suggested (or similar) techniques. Companies should never fall into the trap of adopting the simplest possible solution to this problem: creating a *quota* for the Offshore Center employees in the global awards. Companies might think that creating equal quotas for the HO and Offshore Center employees in the global awards will give fair and equal opportunities to the Offshore Center employees to win the awards. For example, a company might decide that the "Global Employee of the Month" award will be given in a round-robin basis—to Offshore Center employees on alternate months and to HO employees on other alternate months.

The problem with this approach is that in the month an Offshore Center employee is supposed to win the award, all the Offshore Center employees are competing for the award only with their local peer employees. They are not competing with any HO employees, since no HO employee can win the award in that month. The global award then effectively becomes a "local award" for the Offshore Center.

The purpose of instituting global awards is to enable the Offshore Center employees to compete with the HO employees to win the awards, which will make them strive hard and perform beyond their potential. This basic purpose would be defeated if the Offshore Center employees will win global awards without competing with the HO employees. Hence, companies are strongly discouraged from using quotas in deciding on global awards.

* * * * *

An area of major debate in the offshoring industry is the role to be played by the Offshore Center head. At one extreme, some companies give their Offshore Center head complete responsibility, authority, and control over the Offshore Center teams and projects. At the other extreme, some companies run their Offshore Centers without a local head, with all the Offshore Center teams reporting directly to the HO management. Chapter 10 will address the issue of deciding the right role and responsibilities of the Offshore Center head based on multiple factors: the type and size of the company, the size of the Offshore Center and its growth plans, the nature of projects to be offshored, etc. The chapter will describe various functions to be performed by the Offshore Center head, and will show how these functions map to the above factors.

Chapter 10

Roles and Responsibilities of the Offshore Center Head

The role to be played by the Offshore Center head has long been an area of debate. Different companies follow different norms in this respect. At one extreme, some companies capitalize fully on the strengths of their Offshore Center heads by giving them complete responsibility, authority, and control over the Offshore Center teams and projects. At the other extreme, some companies run their Offshore Centers without a local head, with all the Offshore Center teams reporting directly to the head office (HO) management. Further, there are companies where the Offshore Center heads play almost a nominal and ceremonial role, handling only some administrative responsibilities of the Center. This last scenario is usually the most unfortunate scenario, in that the company grossly underutilizes the strengths of its Offshore Center head and thus defeats the basic purpose of creating this position in the first place.

A company typically selects a senior industry professional within the country of its Offshore Center as the head of the Center. He or she generally has extensive experience in managing large teams and successfully running companies in the country. Such a professional can add significant value to the Offshore Center with his or her expertise and experience. However, to meet this objective, the company must judiciously decide the role, authority, and responsibilities of the Offshore Center head position. Since each company has unique characteristics and offshoring requirements, this chapter suggests that companies define the role of the Offshore Center head based on multiple factors—the type and size of the company, the size of the Offshore Center and its growth plans, the company's senior management's knowledge about running a company in the country of the Offshore Center, and the nature of projects to be offshored, ranging from totally independent projects to plain extensions of HO projects.

The chapter starts by elaborating the factors that the company's top management should consider to decide the role, authority, and responsibilities of its Offshore Center head. It then describes various functions performed by a typical Offshore Center head, and shows how these functions map to the above factors. The chapter concludes by suggesting an approach to use to evaluate the performance of the Offshore Center head.

10.1. Factors Determining the Role of the Offshore Center Head

The company top management should decide the role and responsibilities of its Offshore Center head based on the nature of the company, its offshoring strategies, and the challenges being faced in implementing these strategies. The following are some of the factors that should be considered by the company to make the right decision in this respect.

10.1.1. Offshore Center Size and Growth Plans

The company should decide its long-term strategy on the team size and growth plans for its Offshore Center. The decision should be based on factors such as the total size of the company, the number and size of its projects that can be offshored, the cost savings desired from offshoring, etc.

At one end are small companies or start-ups that have a limited number of total employees. Such a company might have an Offshore Center with a small team size and with limited growth plans. Although the team size within the Offshore Center might be small, it could still be a large proportion of the overall team size of the company, since that count itself is small. Hence, the Offshore Center will still be executing a large proportion of projects of the company.

At the other end are large companies running a number of projects with large team sizes. Such a company might set up an Offshore Center with a large team size. It would plan to grow the Offshore Center to a much larger size in the long run by offloading a large number of big projects to the Center. The company will then be able to achieve high cost savings from its Offshore Center. Thus, the major challenge faced by such a company is that it should be able to significantly grow the size of its Offshore Center within a short time span, without compromising the quality of the employees. The key expectations from the Offshore Center head are then to hire a large number of strong candidates from the industry and train them effectively, building their skills in the domain of the projects of the company.

10.1.2. Visibility of the Company in the Country of the Offshore Center

The company should also judge its visibility in the country where it is setting up the Offshore Center. If it is a large global company that markets its products and services across the world, then the company will be well known to professionals in the country of the Offshore Center. Thus, the challenges in hiring professionals for the Offshore Center may not be extremely high, since professionals in that country will be willing to join because of the global reputation of the company.

In contrast, for a small company or a start-up, although it may have good markets and reputation in the country of the HO, it may have absolutely no market presence in the country of the Offshore Center. Such a company will have almost no visibility among the professionals in the country of the Offshore Center. The Offshore Center will thus have problems attracting good professionals from the industry to join the Center.

Since the Offshore Center of such a company may not easily be able to hire professionals directly from the industry, a key expectation from the Offshore Center head should be to have direct contacts with many professionals, who might be persuaded to join the Offshore Center. Further, the Offshore Center head should be expected to build the image of the company within the country of the Offshore Center to be able to attract key industry professionals to join the Center.

10.1.3. Head Office Senior Management's Knowledge of Running a Company in the Country of the Offshore Center

The HO senior management of the company should also make a self-assessment of its understanding and knowledge of establishing and running a company in the country of the Offshore Center. They must realize that their vast knowledge and experience of running a company in their own country may not be exactly relevant to running an Offshore Center in a different country. For example, the most popular job sites, recruitment agencies, and public relations (PR) agencies that are delivering good results for the company in its own country may also have a presence in the country of the Offshore Center, but the HO management should not assume that the same agencies will deliver well for its Offshore Center, since these agencies may not be the leading agencies in the country of the Offshore Center.

Similarly, as was highlighted in Chapter 4, there may be huge differences between the work norms being followed in the HO and the prevalent work norms in the industry of the country of the Offshore Center. The HO management may be unaware of the Offshore Center's work culture, management practices, employee sensitivities, employee career growth expectations, and other related norms.

Thus, if HO senior managers have not been involved previously in setting up and running Offshore Centers in that country (for example, with their previous employers), they must select a strong Offshore Center head with vast industry experience *early in the cycle* of setting up the Center. Such an Offshore Center head can then establish the Center successfully and implement strong local work culture and practices.

10.1.4. Nature of the Projects to Be Offshored

Each company has a vision of the nature of activities/projects it plans to offload to its Offshore Center. The following are some examples of the offshoring visions of companies, with increasing level of responsibilities being handled by the Offshore Center:

1. The Offshore Center is offloaded engineering projects from the HO, but only limited functions within these projects are transferred. For example, suppose the HO develops products and the Offshore Center operates only as a "testing center." The Offshore Center has teams of test professionals to test the products developed in the HO, for compliance to their specifications and for their ability to meet the strict quality requirements of the customers. However, no product development is performed in the Offshore Center.

2. The Offshore Center is assigned complete engineering projects, developing some products of the company for a *selected set of customers*, with responsibility for handling all the functions of design, development, and testing of these products. Customers in different countries may have different requirements for the same category of products. For example, the user interface and features of a mobile application will be different for countries with low-speed 2G mobile data connection and for countries with high-speed 4G connection, and hence different types of products (mobile applications) need to be developed for such countries.

The company can decide that its Offshore Center will perform product development only for the requirements of the company's customers in the country of the Offshore Center (and some neighboring countries), since the Offshore Center team is closer to these customers and understands their requirements better than the teams in the HO. However, the Offshore Center is not offloaded projects for development of any other global products of the company.

3. The Offshore Center is assigned development projects for some of the global products of the company. However, the company offshores only the development of some of its peripheral products, while the responsibility for developing core products still resides with the HO teams.

4. The Offshore Center is involved in development of the core global products of the company without any restrictions, as is being done in the HO. The overall engineering projects for developing these products are executed by distributed global project teams, based in the HO and the Offshore Center. Projects for development of some of these core global products can also be assigned independently to the Offshore Center.

5. The Offshore Center is assigned all the engineering responsibilities described in Point 4 above, and is also additionally assigned major strategic responsibilities of the company. Some of the strategic responsibilities handled by the Offshore Center might include performing the product management functions of conceiving new products to be developed by the company (for product development companies), deciding new business and technology domains in which the company will execute services projects to win new set of customers and generate new avenues of revenue growth (for services companies), and making strategic acquisitions for the company for its inorganic growth, to significantly increase the company size and revenues.

Each of the above set of responsibilities handled by various types of Offshore Centers presents its own unique set of challenges. Companies must ensure that the Offshore Center head to be hired by them has the set of skills and experience to handle the challenges presented by the type and nature of their Offshore Center. As an example, the unique set of challenges faced in an Offshore Center handling responsibilities described in Point 4 above, of executing distributed projects of the company, are discussed next.

Since, in the case of globally distributed projects, a large number of Offshore Center projects are extensions to HO projects, some companies execute all the controlling modules of the overall projects within the HO and run *mere extensions of these projects* in the Offshore Center. The projects in the two locations then become quite closely interlinked. Overall control of all the project modules resides with the HO project managers, and the Offshore Center teams merely execute their extension modules under the control of these HO managers. The Offshore Center project teams are then effectively controlled by the HO management, instead of by the Offshore Center management.

In contrast, some companies have been able to provide significant independence and control over offshored projects to the Offshore Center management. They have offloaded some totally independent projects to the Offshore Center, being managed totally by the Offshore Center project managers. Further, even for the Offshore Center projects that are extensions to the overall projects within the HO, these companies have been able to segregate these projects with a high level of independence. The parts of the projects being executed in the Offshore Center are quite independent, having minimal dependencies on the parts of the projects being executed in the HO. The Offshore Center project teams are then responsible for designing and implementing their projects with minimal dependence on the HO project teams, except for the final integration of their project modules with the HO project modules at the end of the project execution. The Offshore Center projects are then independently managed by their own project managers, who have control over their teams.

A large number of companies have a mix of the above two types of projects in their Offshore Centers, with some closely linked projects being controlled by the HO managers, while other independent projects are managed entirely by the Offshore Center managers.

Each of these project distribution models creates a different set of challenges to be managed by the Offshore Center head. The Offshore Center head is expected to work with the HO management to increase the number of independent projects in the Center, and then lead his or her project managers effectively to deliver on these projects. For closely interlinked projects, the Offshore Center head is expected to establish effective interfaces with the HO managers controlling the Offshore Center teams and ensure full support for the success of their projects by hiring and building strong teams to work on these projects.

10.2. Functions Performed by the Offshore Center Head

Although there are companies that run their Offshore Centers without hiring an on-site head, these instances tend to be short-term arrangements or perhaps suitable only for some specific offshoring goals. A company might decide to start the Offshore Center without a head and use the services of consultant companies to set up the Center. The teams in the Offshore Center would then report directly to the HO managers for all their functions. Such reporting structures may work fine if the size of the Offshore Center is small and there are no plans to grow it to a large size even in the long run. Once the Offshore Center size grows to a critical mass, however, especially if the company plans to grow the Center to a larger size, then a whole range of functions need to be performed to run and grow the Center successfully. The company must then hire a capable and experienced Offshore Center head.

The Offshore Center head can add significant value to the company. He or she is typically a senior industry professional with years of experience running companies successfully and managing large projects/teams in the industry in the country of the Offshore Center. Such a professional can tap on his or her network, expertise, and experience to perform a range of critical functions for the success of the Offshore Center, as detailed in the next sections.

10.2.1. Setting up the Offshore Center

The Offshore Center head is responsible for setting up the Center, if he or she is hired by the company early in the cycle of establishing the Offshore Center. This person first works closely with the HO top management to understand the company's offshoring strategies, its expectations for the Offshore Center, allocated budgets for setting up and running the Center, cost savings expected from offshoring, the business and technical domains of the work of the company, the kinds of projects it plans to offload to the Center, etc. The new head then applies knowledge of setting up and running companies in his or her country to suggest the set of cities that would have the talent available for executing projects in the business and technical domains of work of the company, would allow setting up the Offshore Center within the allocated budget, and would allow the operating costs of the Offshore Center to be low enough to meet the company's cost savings expectations from offshoring.

Once one of these cities is approved by the HO top management, the new head executes the complete number of tasks required to set up the Offshore Center—such as registering the company with the government, getting all legal clearances, renting the office space, setting up requisite infrastructure, handling all administrative and financial aspects of setting up an office, etc.

10.2.2. Representing the Offshore Center to the Head Office Senior Management

The Offshore Center head is the interface of the Offshore Center to the global top management of the company. He or she represents the interests of the Offshore Center to the company top/senior management to win favorable decisions for the Center. He or she is a part of the key global strategic management committees of the company along with the senior management team of the HO. Such committees usually consist of the vice presidents/global heads of the key functions of the company, for example, Engineering, Finance, Human Resources, Product Management, etc. Some of the critical strategic management committees also have company top management personnel including the CEO/president as a member.

These committees decide the long-term strategies of the company, and the role to be played by the Offshore Center in contributing to the success of these strategies. These committees decide strategies including the long-term growth plans of the company, new revenue-generation avenues, new products to be developed (for product development companies), new services domains to be focused on for winning projects (for services companies), cost-saving expectations from offshoring, growth plans for the Offshore Center, etc.

The Offshore Center head participates in these committees to gather a deep understanding of the company strategies and works toward aligning the Offshore Center strategies with them. He or she knows the strengths of the Offshore Center team. He or she gains an in-depth understanding of the business and technical domains of the upcoming projects of the company. He or she highlights to the committee the expertise and experience of the Offshore Center team in executing projects in these domains. He or she also shares knowledge of available talent in the local industry, near the Offshore Center location, including people who have similar expertise and experience. He or she explains the strategy for attracting these professionals to join the Offshore Center and shows that they can be hired within a short time frame. He or she also explains the cost of running these projects in the Offshore Center and compares it with the cost of running them in the HO.

The HO senior management should then be convinced that the Offshore Center has the capability to execute the upcoming projects, can significantly grow its team size within a short time frame to run large-sized projects, and can offer significant cost savings in running these projects as compared to running them in the HO. The HO senior management will then offload many core and large projects to the Offshore Center and agree to more significant growth in the Offshore Center team size than they may have planned earlier.

After winning the projects, the Offshore Center head keeps working closely with these heads of various company functions to ensure overall success of projects with the help of his or her subordinate managers in the Offshore Center.

10.2.3. Managing Offshore Center Engineering Teams

The Offshore Center head has the overall responsibility for the Offshore Center engineering team and their project deliverables. The Offshore Center project managers (/engineering directors), with their subordinate teams, report to the Offshore Center head. The Center head has vast prior experience in managing large teams and can apply effective management practices and project execution techniques to deliver the best results on the projects. He or she understands the strengths, expectations, and career growth aspirations of the Offshore Center employees. He or she applies this knowledge to lead, motivate, and manage the Offshore Center managers, and their teams, effectively, to ensure that their projects are delivered on schedule, meet high quality standards, and achieve high customer satisfaction.

Section 10.1.4 described the activities performed by various types of Offshore Centers. The following are the functions performed by the Offshore Center head for each of them.

1. If the Offshore Center is working purely as a "testing center," testing products being developed in the HO, then the Offshore Center head will typically be a senior test professional who has prior experience of leading and managing testing teams and projects. He or she might have been either the head of a company running testing projects or the head of a testing division of a large company.

   He or she would perform the functions of recruiting experienced test managers and their teams in the Offshore Center, setting up interfaces with the development managers in the HO, transferring the knowledge of products being developed in the HO to the Offshore Center teams, and setting up strong testing processes to ensure that the Offshore Center teams perform stringent testing on these products to meet the high quality expectations of the company.

   Companies should note that selecting a purely test professional as the Offshore Center head works well in the long run if the company plans to keep running the Center as a testing center for its lifetime (or for many years). However, this strategy has pitfalls if the company's vision is to initially run only testing projects in the Offshore Center and then, over a period of time, expand the activities of the Center to perform complete product development and testing projects. The transition to this expanded role for the Offshore Center can sometimes be painful for the Offshore Center head, and also for the company.

   Once the company decides to expand the role of the Offshore Center, the HO vice president for engineering will generally recruit a new Offshore Center head who has expertise and experience in managing both development and testing teams. The current Offshore Center head is then relegated to the role of being just a director of testing under the new Offshore Center head. This person then feels unhappy at losing the Center head role and might decide to quit the company.

The Offshore Center then loses a highly capable senior-level manager who has extensive experience of the company's products and project teams. If the company wants to avoid such an unfortunate scenario, it should set the expectations of this test professional right, at the time of initially recruiting him or her as the Offshore Center head. He or she can be informed that his or her role is to be head of the test division of the Offshore Center and he or she will temporarily also play the role of the Offshore Center head, until a new head is hired after transition of the Offshore Center from being purely a testing center to being a full-fledged development and testing center. He or she will then not be upset at losing the Offshore Center head position later.

Another possible option is for the vice president to judge the management capabilities of this test professional over a period of time, during the period he or she is managing the Offshore Center teams as the temporary Center head. If the vice president assesses that the person has very strong capabilities and has the ability to learn new domains, then the vice president may consider continuing with the same person as the Offshore Center head even after the Center transitions to a full-fledged development and testing center. The vice president can start adding small development projects to the Offshore Center and slowly increase their sizes; can mentor and train the person on this additional responsibility of managing a development division; and recruit experienced development managers under the person to manage the development projects. The vice president can then evaluate the performance of the person in delivering on these development projects, and if the performance is found satisfactory, then the vice president may decide to continue the person as the Offshore Center head even after the transition happens in the Center. However, if the person is unable to deliver on these small development projects, then the relegation of the person from the Offshore Center head position would be unavoidable.

2. If the Offshore Center is assigned complete engineering projects of developing some products of the company catering only to the requirements of the customers local to the country of the Offshore Center, then the Offshore Center head will typically be a senior professional who has experience of managing teams executing full-fledged projects involving design, development, and testing functions. He or she will utilize his or her knowledge of the requirements of the local customers and lead the Offshore Center teams effectively to develop and deliver products for these customers.

3. If the Offshore Center is assigned development of only some peripheral products of the company, then the company can hire a Center head with

prior experience in managing small teams executing simple projects. Obviously, the expertise and experience expected from this person will be less than those of a professional with experience in managing large, complex, and core projects. Thus, hiring such a Center head would also not be too costly for the company.

However, as discussed in Chapter 7, offloading only low-revenue-generating small and peripheral projects to the Offshore Center results in gross underutilization of the talent of its teams, and significantly limits the Center's contributions to the company's revenues and cost savings. Hence, even if a company initially decides to use the Offshore Center only for executing peripheral projects, it is strongly recommended to out-grow this model over a period of time and start offloading large core projects to the Center.

Keeping in mind such long-term plans for the Offshore Center, the company should hire a very senior industry professional as their Offshore Center head, from the time of establishing the Center itself. This professional should have a high level of expertise and extensive experience in managing large, core, and complex projects. Since this person will have much greater capabilities than those required to lead teams to deliver on peripheral projects, he or she should initially lead the Offshore Center teams easily to deliver on its peripheral projects with a high success rate. Thus, he or she will be able to create a highly positive impression on the HO management about the capabilities of the Offshore Center. He or she could then use the techniques suggested in Chapter 7 to convince the HO management to offload large, core, and complex projects to the Offshore Center—by hiring highly capable and experienced professionals from the industry with expertise in the domains of the projects of the company, getting advance information about upcoming core projects of the company, training the Offshore Center teams on the domains and technologies of these projects, and winning these core projects from the HO by highlighting these strengths to the HO management.

The Offshore Center will then also be executing high-revenue-generating core and large projects of the company and will contribute much more significantly to the revenues and profits of the company, as compared to working only on small and peripheral projects.

4. If the Offshore Center is assigned development of global products of the company without any restrictions, as is being done in the HO, then the Offshore Center head should have the expertise and extensive experience of managing teams executing large, core, and complex globally distributed projects. He or she should have experience in leading offshore teams executing extensions of projects being executed in the HO of companies.

He or she will be able to use this expertise to interface successfully with the company's HO management to ensure success of the components of their overall projects being executed in the Offshore Center. Since these projects will be developing products for global customers, he or she will be able to use his or her deep understanding of the requirements of global customers to ensure that the deliverables from the Offshore Center meet their expectations from such products, and meet their stringent quality norms.

At the end of Section 10.1, some of the unique challenges presented by such globally distributed projects were discussed. The means to be adopted by the Offshore Center head to meet these challenges will be discussed later in this section.

5. If the Offshore Center is not limited to handling only engineering functions, but is also playing a strategic role for the company, then the company should hire an Offshore Center head with expertise and experience in handling strategic responsibilities in addition to being able to lead engineering teams. For example, if the company expects the Offshore Center to strategize and conceive new products, then the Offshore Center head should have expertise and experience in establishing product management teams, working with these teams to approach global customers and understand their product requirements, understand the features of similar product offerings from competing companies, and decide new products with comprehensive feature-sets that can succeed in the market.

For example, such a company may decide to hire a past entrepreneur, who has successfully run a company developing products for global customers as the Offshore Center head, since he or she will possess strategic understanding of the markets and launching the right products for it. The Offshore Center head can then work closely with the HO top management/senior management to ensure that the Offshore Center makes significant strategic contributions to the company, such as conceiving new products, deciding new domains in which the company will execute services projects, and making strategic acquisitions for the company.

This topic will be discussed more in detail in Chapter 12.

Section 10.1.4 gave examples of the unique challenges faced in Offshore Centers that are executing distributed projects of the company. It will now be discussed how the Offshore Center head can use his or her expertise in managing these challenges.

Since projects in the Offshore Center are often extensions to core projects being executed in the HO, the Offshore Center head should be able to work closely with the HO management to implement the same set of project methodologies, processes, and documentation standards across both the Offshore Center and HO.

Suppose the HO offloads a mix of independent projects and projects that are extensions to core HO projects to the Offshore Center. The Offshore Center project managers have complete authority and responsibility for their teams executing independent projects. The Offshore Center teams are fully responsible for design and implementation of such projects. Successful delivery of such independent projects results in growth of the project teams within the Offshore Center only, since no teams in the HO are involved in these projects. Thus, the aim of the Offshore Center head should be to maximize winning independent projects for the Offshore Center, since then the teams will get opportunities to work on core and large projects, and the Offshore Center can grow to a larger size.

However, it is a reality that few such independent projects exist in offshoring scenarios. A large number of projects in the Offshore Center are extensions to core overall projects being executed in the HO. The Offshore Center head, along with subordinate project managers and technical architects in the Center, works closely with the overall project heads (managers) and technical architects in the HO to ensure that the project modules to be offloaded to the Offshore Center are as independent of the HO core project modules as possible. The overall project is then redesigned in a highly modular fashion, with minimal interdependencies between various project modules. The Offshore Center project modules are then mostly independent except for having well-defined interfaces with the HO core project modules with which these modules will be integrated at the end of the project execution.

Thus, Offshore Center project managers are then managing their project modules independently, and their teams are responsible for all functions for these project modules—design, implementation, testing, and final integration with the HO core project modules. The interfacing and integration of the Offshore Center and HO project modules is coordinated by the program management team. Thus, following such an approach, the Offshore Center head ensures that a large proportion of the projects in the Center are mostly independent projects.

The rest of the projects in the Offshore Center might be extensions to core HO projects. The HO project managers are then controlling and managing the Offshore Center teams working on their extension project modules, and no Offshore Center project managers are involved in these projects. The Offshore Center head ensures that proper reporting mechanisms and interfaces are established between these Offshore Center teams and HO managers to ensure the success of these projects.

However, even though these extension projects are not managed within the Offshore Center, one should not assume that the Offshore Center head plays only a minimal role in leading these project teams. These Offshore Center teams are reporting to their HO project managers for the *project-related purpose* only.

The Offshore Center head is still responsible for all the other core functions related to these teams, such as hiring, training, skill building, compensation planning, etc. The HO project managers cannot handle these functions, since they are not equipped to handle such tasks for the Offshore Center. HO managers are not knowledgeable about the norms and mechanisms to be followed for such functions in the country of the Offshore Center and, hence, look to the Offshore Center head to perform these functions. The Offshore Center head then hires, builds, and retains strong Offshore Center teams for the projects of these HO project managers.

Thus, the Offshore Center head is responsible for the complete Offshore Center engineering team, working on both independent and distributed projects.

10.2.4. Building the Image of the Offshore Center in Its Country

As a company sets up its Offshore Center, its first and most important task is to make the company's name visible and to make industry professionals aware of the company having started an Offshore Center in their country. This activity of publicizing the name of the company's Offshore Center and its achievements must remain a continuous activity throughout the existence of the Center, both for Offshore Centers of globally reputed large companies and those of small companies/start-ups.

If the Offshore Center wants to attract management and technical professionals from the industry who are working in the company's domain of work, it must build its positive image among these professionals. The Offshore Center reaches out to these professionals through various forums to highlight the positive facts about the company—the company's high global standing, global success of products developed, names of leading global clients for which the company is executing services projects, the business and technical domains of the projects being executed by the company, the high-end advanced technologies being used in the projects, the complexity of its products/projects and the challenges being offered to the employees working on them, the key deliverables and achievements of the Offshore Center, intellectual property rights developed and patents granted to the Offshore Center, employee-friendly policies, attractive compensation/perks, etc.

The Offshore Center head has long years of industry experience, which has made this person aware of the right approach to be used for publicizing the company's Offshore Center's name, the right PR agency/media contacts to be used, the right forums to be used, etc. He or she uses vast experience and contacts to build the image of the company's Offshore Center by using multiple means.

1. He or she participates in the activities of various CEO forums of companies similar to this company and makes positive contributions in various initiatives run by these forums. Such forums and their initiatives receive excellent media coverage, and hence, the name of the company's Offshore Center becomes visible in the country.

2. He or she is well aware of the PR agencies that can get the message about the Offshore Center across to the right print publications, digital/ mobile portals, and broadcast media channels that are watched by professionals interested in the domain of work of the company. He or she uses the services of these PR agencies so he or she can be interviewed. He or she obtains positive stories about the Offshore Center published on these channels. He or she has also developed some direct contacts with some media channels and uses them too to publicize the name of the Offshore Center.

3. He or she is active in a number of professional bodies of technical and management professionals, such as the Project Management Institute (PMI), the Institute of Electrical and Electronics Engineers (IEEE), the Association for Computing Machinery (ACM), etc. He or she is aware of the bodies that have the maximum participation of industry professionals relevant to the Offshore Center. This awareness enables him or her to actively promote the name of the Offshore Center by sponsoring events of these professional bodies and encouraging his or her team to write articles in publications of these bodies and presenting papers at their conferences.

Section 10.1.2 discussed the Offshore Center of a small company, or a startup, that has almost no visibility among the professionals in the country of the Offshore Center. The global top management of such a company should hire the Offshore Center head very early in the cycle, almost at the time the Offshore Center is established. The Offshore Center head will then build the image of the company, and its Offshore Center, and make it highly visible among professionals relevant to the Center. Thus, the Offshore Center will be able to attract experienced and capable professionals to join it.

In the absence of an Offshore Center head, the Center will keep operating with limited visibility. Only a few industry professionals will then be interested in applying for jobs in the Center. The Offshore Center will then be unable to attract and hire quality talent, severely impacting the deliverables of the Center.

10.2.5. Attracting Talent to Grow the Offshore Center's Size

The Offshore Center head is responsible for growing the size of the Center by attracting quality management and technical talent with experience relevant to the business and technology domains of the company. He or she achieves this objective by some of the following means.

1. The above-described efforts in building the image of the Offshore Center in various media channels will make the Offshore Center and its work visible to industry professionals. The active promotion of the Offshore Center among various professional bodies of management and technology professionals will create a positive image about the Center among the members of these bodies who are working in the domain of work of the company. Thus, professionals relevant to the domain of work of the Offshore Center will become interested in applying for opportunities and joining the Center.

2. Companies usually hire senior professionals through recruitment agencies. There will be a large number of recruitment agencies in the country of the Offshore Center. The Offshore Center head has been hiring through various recruitment agencies for many years and has developed top-level contacts at these agencies. Based on his or her experience, he or she will be well aware of the recruitment agencies that have shown positive results in getting experienced professionals relevant to the domain of work of the company. He or she will approach only such relevant recruiters to hire experienced and quality professionals for the Offshore Center.

   In the absence of an Offshore Center head, the HO management may make the mistake of approaching either only the large recruitment agencies or the regional offices (in the country of the Offshore Center) of global recruitment agencies that have shown good results in the country of the HO. However, both of these approaches may fail to achieve the desired results, since these recruitment agencies may not have candidates relevant to the domain of work of the company *in the country of the Offshore Center.*

3. Besides hiring experienced professionals, the Offshore Center also needs to hire new graduates through campus recruitment. Although companies are generally aware of the top professional colleges, not all of these colleges may be relevant to the Offshore Center because of constraints such as salaries being offered by the visiting companies to the students of some colleges being much beyond the reach of the Offshore Center, the majority of students of some colleges being unwilling to relocate to the city of the Offshore Center because they are residents of a distant city/state/region where they can easily get job opportunities, etc. The Offshore Center head is aware of the professional colleges from which strong and interested graduates can be hired *within the salary norms decided by the company for graduates* and who will be willing to work in the city of

the Offshore Center. He or she has built good relations with such colleges over the years and will tap this network to build a positive image among the students of these colleges about the challenging work being done by the Offshore Center. This objective will be achieved by sponsoring college events, making company presentations to students, etc. These efforts will allow the Offshore Center to get a high rank among companies approaching these colleges for campus recruitment to be able to hire high-quality students.

4. The Offshore Center head has been working in the industry for many years and has established personal contacts with many management and technical professionals. He or she is personally aware of the capabilities of these professionals and uses these contacts to invite some of these capable professionals to join the Offshore Center. Since these professionals have faith in his or her leadership qualities, they will be more willing to join the Center.

Section 10.1.2 discussed the Offshore Center of a small company or a start-up that has almost no visibility among the professionals in the country of the Offshore Center. The mode of hiring through personal contacts of the Offshore Center head is much more critical for such an Offshore Center in its initial phase, since otherwise only a few good professionals from the industry will be interested in joining an unknown company. As time passes, the Offshore Center head will be able to build a positive image about the company, and then other methods of hiring, as discussed above, will also start yielding results.

Once the Offshore Center head has been able to attract good candidates to apply for positions in the Center, the next challenge will be to match their salary expectations to enable them join the Center. It was discussed in Chapter 8 that highly experienced and capable candidates demand salaries that can be much above the salary cap decided by the company for their job positions. It was mentioned there that the Offshore Center management should convince the HO management to relax the salary caps for such excellent candidates, by showing them that the higher salaries will be an investment that will result in much higher cost savings in the future, due to many more large and core projects being executed in the Offshore Center because of the presence of such capable employees. The detailed steps to be taken by the Offshore Center head for convincing the HO management for this purpose are discussed next.

Let us take the example of hiring an excellent expert in the technology domain of some of the core projects of the company. The Offshore Center head performs a number of tasks to convince the HO management to relax the salary cap for hiring this candidate.

1. Since the Offshore Center head has been working closely with the HO vice president for engineering and the product management head, he or she is aware of the future products to be developed and the future core and large projects to be executed by the company. Then, with the help of senior technical personnel in the Offshore Center, he or she gains knowledge of the technologies to be used in these projects. Next, the Offshore Center head makes a judgment on which of these core projects fall within the technology expertise of the candidate being hired and can be executed by building teams around him or her.

2. The Offshore Center head estimates the size and composition of teams to be built around the candidate for executing these core projects in the Offshore Center. He or she makes projections of the cost to be incurred in executing these projects in the Offshore Center, based on the estimated salaries and all the other project-related expenses of these teams.

3. Next, he or she gathers inputs from the HO vice president for engineering and HO finance head on the expenses being incurred in the HO on salaries and project-related expenses of their teams. Based on these inputs, he or she projects the cost of executing the same projects in the HO.

4. He or she calculates the difference in the cost of executing the projects in the HO and the cost of executing the same projects in the Offshore Center. Then, this cost differential is compared with the projected increase in the expenses of the Offshore Center that are due to the high salary being offered to this candidate. The Offshore Center head then demonstrates to the HO management that the long-term cost saving achieved by being able to execute more core and large projects in the Offshore Center, because of the presence of this expert, offsets the higher salary cost by multiple factors.

   Thus, he or she is able to convince the HO management to relax the hard salary caps and is able to hire excellent talent at the salaries expected by such candidates.

10.2.6. Training and Skill Building of Offshore Center Teams

The Offshore Center head is aware of the right trainers who can impart management and technical training relevant to the domain of projects being executed in the Offshore Center. Then the Center head organizes external trainings for his or her employees by these trainers to improve their skills, productivity, and delivery capabilities. Further, the Center head conducts internal training sessions for his or her subordinate managers by sharing experiences of managing large teams for many years.

It was mentioned in Chapter 8 that Offshore Centers are constrained by limited training budgets. The chapter stressed the need for the Offshore Center management to convince the HO management to relax the hard upper limits on these budgets. It was suggested that this task should be accomplished by arguing that higher training budgets are an investment that will produce much higher benefits to the company in the long run—by increasing company revenues due to improved employee productivity and by reducing company costs by shortening project delivery cycles. The Offshore Center head guides subordinate managers in this process of estimating the higher training budgets needed and projects the long-term benefits of these investments. Once the budgeting exercise is complete for all the subordinate managers and their teams, the Offshore Center head collates all the data to estimate the overall training budget for the Offshore Center.

The task of convincing the HO management of the need for this higher training budget will require strong negotiation skills, which the Offshore Center managers may not necessarily possess, especially if they are not very experienced managers. Since the Offshore Center head is much more experienced in these matters, he or she assumes this responsibility and uses his or her excellent negotiation skills to convince the HO management of the need for an increased training budget.

Chapter 8 also mentioned that the Offshore Center needs to make increased investments in hardware and software resources to train its employees on advanced technologies being used in the core projects of the company. The Offshore Center head handles the responsibility of convincing the HO management to have a single engineering budget head across the HO and Offshore Center to acquire these resources and overcome budgetary constraints imposed on the Offshore Center.

10.2.7. Building the Offshore Center's Local Work Culture

It was discussed in Chapter 4 that although the Offshore Center should integrate with the HO on projects-related matters, it should still retain its local work culture. It was suggested that a local management committee of Offshore Center managers should be formed to make decisions on the Offshore Center policies, work culture, management practices, employee career growth norms and designations, as per the norms being followed in the country of the Offshore Center.

The Offshore Center head chairs this local management committee. He or she guides the committee members in making their decisions and makes the final decision. Further, based on his or her years of experience in running companies, the Offshore Center head can select the best management practices of these companies and adopt them in the Offshore Center.

Section 10.1.3 discussed the case where the Offshore Center may belong to a company where the HO senior management has limited knowledge of the prevalent work culture and norms in the country of the Offshore Center. Such a company should hire its Offshore Center head as early as possible in establishing the Center. Such an approach enables the Center head to implement the local work culture, as per the norms of the country of the Offshore Center, from the inception of the Center.

If the Offshore Center head is not hired early, then the HO management initially imposes the work culture of the country of the HO on the Offshore Center, possibly resulting in resentment and demoralization in the Offshore Center teams. The HO management may realize their mistake in the long run and then agree to allow the Offshore Center to have its own work culture and norms, but by then significant damage will have been done to the Center and its employees.

10.2.8. Representing the Interests of the Offshore Center in Global Committees

As mentioned in Chapter 6, companies create a number of global management committees to decide various issues that impact the company as a whole, both the HO and the Offshore Center. Some examples given were committees for deciding overall company policies, management practices, employee appraisal norms, employee benefits, distribution of teams among various locations, resolution of interlocation contention among employees, selection of employees for global top positions, etc. Since the decisions made by such committees have a significant impact on the Offshore Center teams, the committees must have a strong representation from the Offshore Center to discuss the interests of the Center and its employees.

These committees generally consist only of senior management personnel of the company at vice president level (or above) in the company's global hierarchy. If the committee has such senior personnel from the HO, then the Offshore Center representative must also be at a similar level in the company. Since the Offshore Center head is at the vice president level in the global hierarchy of the company, he or she represents the Offshore Center in these committees. He or she is dealing only with his or her peers in the committee meetings and can put across the case of the Offshore Center strongly without any fear. Further, he or she has the expertise and the requisite negotiation skills to present the case of the Offshore Center objectively and convince the committee members to make favorable decisions for the Offshore Center.

If a company is running its Offshore Center without a head, then the representative from the Offshore Center in these committees will be junior to the

HO members of the committees and will not be their peer. Such a committee composition will create an imbalance in favor of the HO, since the Offshore Center representative will fail to represent the interests of the Center strongly enough to win favorable decisions. Thus, most of the decisions of the committees will be tilted against the Offshore Center, as was discussed in Case Study 6.1.

10.2.9. Expediting Offshore Center Decision Making

The Offshore Center head can expedite all the local decisions to make the Center run in an agile fashion. Since the Center head will be the final authority on approving decisions related to all the functions of the Offshore Center, all decisions can be implemented without any delays.

In the absence of an Offshore Center head, all decisions of the Center will have to wait for a long time to be approved by multiple authorities in the HO, which can impact the functioning of the Center adversely. The Offshore Center will then work in an inefficient manner.

For example, it was discussed in Case Study 3.1 that if the decisions on hiring of candidates in the Offshore Center need approval of HO authorities, this can entail inordinate delays. Since excellent candidates often have multiple job offers in hand, they want companies to make their decisions fast so they can decide their career move. Because of long delays in decision making, the Offshore Center may fail to hire such good talent. Such situations can be avoided if the Offshore Center has a local head who can finalize such decisions locally.

10.2.10. Overall Responsibility of the Offshore Center Support Functions

The Offshore Center head has overall responsibility for all the support functions in the Center, such as finance, human resources, administration, system administration, etc. He or she recruits and builds strong teams for each of the functions, with the respective heads of these functions reporting to him or her.

10.3. Evaluating the Performance of the Offshore Center Head

The company's top management should evaluate the performance of the Offshore Center head based on the results shown on the complete gamut of functions the Center head performs as elaborated in the previous section. The top management should assign measurable objectives to the Offshore Center head for each of these functions. The results shown against each of the objectives should be measured to rate the performance of the Offshore Center head.

However, the top management of some companies tends not to follow such an intricate process of performance appraisal but uses a much simpler approach instead. They think that since the Offshore Center is executing parts of the overall projects being controlled from the HO, the core responsibility of the Offshore Center head is to support the overall project heads in the HO in the success of their projects. Thus, the top management just seeks feedback from the HO managers (overall project heads) on how satisfied they are with the support provided by the Offshore Center head on the overall projects being managed by them. The top management then rates the performance of the Offshore Center head based *solely* on this feedback received from these HO managers.

Unfortunately, this approach for judging the performance of the Offshore Center head is inherently flawed. The Offshore Center head is responsible for significantly growing the size of the Center to reduce the costs of the company. However, an increase in the size of the project teams in the Offshore Center may create insecurities in the HO managers, since the size of their direct-reporting local HO project teams become smaller compared to the large Offshore Center project teams. These HO managers then fear losing their role, responsibilities, and authority to the Offshore Center managers in the long run, if the size of the Offshore Center project teams keeps increasing significantly while HO project team sizes remain static at lower numbers. Thus, the HO managers may consider the Offshore Center head's capability to convince the top management in offshoring larger and more projects as a "negative" trait. These HO managers may then give negative feedback on the Offshore Center head to the top management during his or her performance appraisal.

Growing the size of the Offshore Center is the key objective of its head. If the Offshore Center head is working strongly toward meeting this objective, then he or she will be able to grow project team sizes of most of the projects offloaded to the Center, displeasing a large number of HO overall project heads. Thus, the more successful the Offshore Center head has been in meeting his or her key objective, the more it may lead to a larger number of HO managers giving negative feedback about him or her to the top management. The top management then believes that since many HO managers are not satisfied with the performance of the Offshore Center head, he or she must be a low performer and consequently rate his or her performance low. Thus, the Offshore Center head is *penalized* for showing excellent results on his or her core objective!

Thus, the top management must, instead, evaluate the performance of the Offshore Center head based on the results shown on all his or her objectives, and not based solely on feedback from the HO managers. Although aiding and supporting HO managers is an important function of the Offshore Center head, it should be considered as *just one of the many criteria* that are used to evaluate performance. The top management should specifically ask the HO managers if the Offshore Center head has grown the size of the offshore team of their overall projects, and that should be considered as a positive trait when evaluating the performance of the Center head.

Interestingly, the very companies that place significant focus on the feedback of HO managers in judging the performance of the Offshore Center head fail to seek the feedback of the Offshore Center head and the Offshore Center management when evaluating the performance of these HO managers. The company must realize that the overall project heads in the HO need to support the Offshore Center project managers and project teams in multiple fashions to ensure the success of the Offshore Center components of their overall projects. The HO project heads need to work closely with the Offshore Center project managers to distribute appropriate project components to their teams, ensure a smooth transfer of knowledge of the projects to these Offshore Center project teams, regularly interface and communicate with these teams throughout project execution to ensure alignment of the Offshore Center project components with the HO project components, ensure smooth integration of both these project components at the end of the project, act as an interface for the Offshore Center project managers to the external entities related to the projects such as the customers and the product management teams, etc.

Each of these functions is critical to the success of the project components being executed in the Offshore Center. The HO senior management must set measurable objectives for the HO managers, working as overall project heads, for each of these functions. The results shown by the HO managers on these objectives should be considered among the criteria used to evaluate their performance. One criterion to judge the performance of the HO managers should be the feedback received from the Offshore Center head and managers on the level of support provided to the Offshore Center by the HO managers in the smooth transfer and execution of their project components.

Thus, the HO managers will then be motivated to provide extensive support to the Offshore Center teams on their project components. The Offshore Center head and managers will then get the requisite support to ensure the success of the Offshore Center projects.

* * * * *

HO managers sometimes visit the Offshore Center for short-term or long-term expatriate assignments to accomplish specific tasks. These managers sometimes wrongly assume that their skills and working methods being used in handling their current management responsibilities in the HO will suffice in handling their expatriate assignments. These HO managers then fail to deliver on their expatriate assignments. Chapter 11 will show that the roles and responsibilities of an expatriate manager are different from his or her normal management responsibilities within the HO. The chapter will describe the expectations from various types of expatriate assignments and will suggest the new skills and knowledge the HO managers need to gain to prepare for handling these assignments. These techniques will allow expatriate managers to succeed in their assignments and add significant value to the Offshore Center teams, beyond just performing project management activities.

Chapter 11

Being an Expatriate Manager from the Head Office to the Offshore Center

Head office (HO) managers sometimes need to go to the Offshore Center on short-term or long-term expatriate assignments to accomplish specific tasks. Some examples of expatriate assignments are a project team in the Offshore Center initiating work on implementing some components of an overall project of the company, and the concerned overall project head from the HO traveling to the Offshore Center to transfer knowledge about the project to this offshore project team; a company with multiple product development divisions deciding to offshore some projects of one of the divisions to the Offshore Center, and the product development division engineering director from the HO traveling to the Offshore Center to set up the offshore division for that product; and a company deciding to set up an Offshore Center and initially sending a HO senior management person as expatriate Offshore Center head until a local head is hired, and the requisite knowledge is transferred.

The HO management personnel selected as expatriate managers for the above assignments sometimes wrongly assume that their skills, experience, and working methods as used in handling their current management roles in the HO will suffice in handling their expatriate assignments. These HO managers must realize that the roles and responsibilities of an expatriate manager are different from their normal management responsibilities within the HO. This chapter describes the differences in these roles and elaborates the new skills and knowledge the HO managers need to gain to prepare for handling their expatriate assignments. These techniques will allow HO managers to add significant value to the Offshore Center teams beyond just project management activities. Thus, these HO managers will succeed in meeting the expectations of the Offshore Center teams as expatriate managers.

The chapter starts by describing the roles and responsibilities of expatriate managers with some examples of short-term and long-term expatriate assignments. It then describes the preparations to be made by HO managers before starting their expatriate assignments. Since a HO manager will have gained extensive knowledge about the Offshore Center teams after completion of his or her expatriate assignment, the chapter suggests a possible additional role to perform after a return to the HO, to keep adding significant value to the Offshore Center teams. The chapter concludes by describing some possible mistakes that companies should avoid while planning expatriate assignments of HO managers.

11.1. Roles and Responsibilities of an Expatriate Manager

The roles and responsibilities of a HO manager posted as an expatriate manager in the Offshore Center are different from the usual management responsibilities being handled by this person in the HO. Further, these responsibilities and the duration of the expatriate assignment vary according to the nature of the assignment. This section lists three possible expatriate assignments and describes the responsibilities of the expatriate manager in each of these assignments.

11.1.1. Transferring Knowledge of a Head Office Overall Project to the Offshore Center

A number of projects in the Offshore Center are extensions to the overall projects running in the HO. The overall project may initially be running totally within the HO, and the company then decides to offload some of its components to the Offshore Center. A project team under a manager in the Offshore Center is assigned to execute these offshore project components. This Offshore Center team needs to gain knowledge of the overall project and their project components to get started.

The HO manager acting as the overall project head for the project is responsible for transferring the knowledge of the project to this Offshore Center project manager and his or her team. Thus, the HO manager travels to the Offshore Center for a short-term expatriate assignment for this purpose. He or she is accompanied by the overall technical architect of the project.

They perform the following tasks during their stay in the Offshore Center.

1. The HO architect transfers knowledge about the overall project architecture and design to the Offshore Center technical team. He or she describes the division of the overall project into multiple modules and trains the team on the project modules to be executed in the Offshore Center. He or she clearly specifies the interfaces of the Offshore Center project modules with the HO project modules to facilitate a smooth integration of these modules.

2. Since the project modules in the two locations are parts of the same project, the expatriate HO manager works with the Offshore Center manager to implement the same set of project execution methodologies, delivery processes, and documentation standards in the Offshore Center project as are being followed in the HO project. If the company (or the division of the company to which this project belongs to) has already standardized the same set of project execution norms to be followed across both locations for all the projects, then this activity may be limited to standardizing on any nuanced norms being followed in this specific project, which are different from the overall umbrella norms being followed across all the projects in the company.

3. The HO manager and the Offshore Center manager jointly decide the intermediate milestones of the project, expected deliverables at each milestone, and the tasks to be performed at the end of the project execution to integrate the Offshore Center project modules with the HO project modules.

4. The HO manager introduces the Offshore Center manager to the program management team for the overall project in the HO, establishes the communication mechanisms between the Offshore Center manager and team with the program management team, specifies the project tracking mechanisms to be followed, specifies the frequency of project tracking meetings, etc. In fact, the HO manager will also run a few of these inter-location project tracking meetings while based in the Offshore Center itself, with participation of the Offshore Center manager and relevant team members and with remote participation of the program management team and relevant HO project team members from the HO's location.

The HO manager and architect end their expatriate assignment after performing the above tasks of transferring the project knowledge and establishing appropriate interlocation project tracking and interfacing mechanisms to be followed.

11.1.2. Establishing a Division in the Offshore Center

It was mentioned in Chapter 6 that some product companies develop multiple products. Such a company will have multiple product divisions with each division headed by the vice president for engineering for that division (see Figure 6-1). Initially, all these product divisions are based entirely in the HO. After setting up the Offshore Center, the company establishes extensions of these product divisions in the Offshore Center.

Once the vice president of a product division decides to set up the extension of his or her division in the Offshore Center, he or she sends one of his or her subordinate engineering directors as an expatriate to the Offshore Center to perform this task. This is a long-term expatriate assignment during which he or she performs the following set of tasks.

1. He or she works with the Offshore Center head and the human resources division to hire relevant management and technical talent from the industry to build the initial team to start the product division extension in the Offshore Center.
2. He or she heads this Offshore Center team and is responsible for leading, motivating, and managing the team to deliver on their project deliverables. He or she also initiates the process of hiring a local engineering director in the Offshore Center, as early in the cycle as possible. Once the local engineering director comes on board, the expatriate HO engineering director trains and grooms him or her on the tasks to be performed to head the product division extension in the Offshore Center. A sufficient overlap period is provided between the two of them during the period of expatriate assignment for the necessary knowledge to be successfully transferred.
3. The expatriate HO engineering director transfers knowledge about the product, its features, markets, key customers, and the details of competing products to the Offshore Center team.
4. He or she broadly describes the various projects being executed in the HO to build the product and shares details of the specific projects whose extensions are being transferred to the Offshore Center. The project knowledge of each of these projects is then transferred to the relevant

Offshore Center project team by calling the overall project head of the project from the HO on an expatriate assignment, as was described in the previous section.

5. All the projects being executed in a product division usually follow the same project execution norms. He or she implements the same set of project execution methodologies, delivery processes, and documentation standards in the product division extension within the Offshore Center as are being followed in the product division in the HO.

6. The Offshore Center team needs regular inputs from the product management team of the product regarding the product features/requirements, prioritization among various features being implemented in the Offshore Center, ongoing requirement changes, customer feedback on intermediate releases, etc. The expatriate HO engineering director introduces the Offshore Center team to the product management team for the product in HO, establishes the communication mechanisms between the hired Offshore Center engineering director and team with the product management team, decides the modes of communication and information dissemination between them, specifies the frequency of their meetings, etc.

7. After the expatriate HO engineering director has successfully accomplished all the above tasks and has brought the local engineering director up to speed on his or her role and responsibilities, the expatriate HO engineering director can return from his or her expatriate assignment. The local engineering director then takes over the responsibility of heading the extension product division in the Offshore Center.

11.1.3. Setting Up and Operating the Offshore Center

Some companies decide to set up and initially operate their Offshore Centers without hiring a local head. The company usually sends a senior management person from the HO on a long-term expatriate assignment to the Offshore Center to establish and operate the center. This person works with some local consulting companies in the country of the Offshore Center to establish the center. He or she then heads the Offshore Center for a limited period of time and performs all the functions expected from an Offshore Center head, as elaborated in the previous chapter.

The last section discussed how an expatriate HO product division engineering director hires and trains the product division team in the Offshore Center, transfers the product knowledge to this team, shares knowledge of projects being transferred to the Offshore Center, implements the same set of project execution norms in the Offshore Center as are being followed in the HO, and establishes interfaces of the Offshore Center management with various HO entities such as the product management and program management teams of the product division. The expatriate Offshore Center head works in a similar fashion and performs all these tasks *for all the product divisions* of the company being set up in the Offshore Center. He is aided by the various HO product division heads/HO engineering directors in the process.

Further, he or she also sets up all the support divisions in the Offshore Center and establishes their interfaces with the heads of these support divisions in the HO, for example, the vice presidents for finance, human resources, system administration, etc.

He or she keeps running the Offshore Center for a limited period of time and then hires a local head for the center. Similar to the previous section, he or she trains and grooms this local Offshore Center head on the tasks to be performed while heading and running the center. A sufficient overlap period is provided between him or her and the local Offshore Center head during the period of the expatriate assignment for complete knowledge to be successfully transferred. The expatriate Offshore Center head establishes direct contacts between the local head and the company's top/senior management team in the HO, for the local head to get the requisite support to successfully perform all his or her tasks. The expatriate Offshore Center head then completes his or her expatriate assignment and returns to the HO. The local Offshore Center head then takes over responsibility for running the center.

11.2. Preparation Required for the Expatriate Manager Role

The role and responsibilities of an expatriate manager are different from the usual project management responsibilities handled by the managers in the HO. An expatriate manager is expected to add significant value to the Offshore Center beyond the typical project management activities. A HO manager selected for expatriate assignment must recognize these differences in expectations from his or her expatriate role as compared to his or her current management role in the HO. He or she should improve his or her knowledge and skills to be able to successfully deliver the responsibilities of his or her expatriate assignment.

The following are some of the expectations from an expatriate manager along with description of how a HO manager can prepare himself or herself to meet these expectations, before starting his or her expatriate assignment.

1. The core requirement from an expatriate manager is that he or she must be a thorough expert on the project/product to be transferred to the

Offshore Center. In case of a short-term expatriate assignment of starting the extension of an HO project in the Offshore Center, the overall project head should be sent, since he or she will be fully knowledgeable about the project. He or she can use his or her knowledge to transfer the complete project details to the Offshore Center team and can answer all their queries.

However, in case of starting a product division extension in the Offshore Center, the head of the product division in the HO, namely, the vice president for engineering for that product, cannot go on the expatriate assignment. The assignment is of a long duration, and he or she needs to be based in the HO on a continuing basis to head the ongoing product development and to interface with various internal/external stakeholders related to the product. Thus, typically he or she will send one of his or her subordinate engineering directors on the assignment, with the HO team of this engineering director reporting locally to the vice president during the term of the assignment (along with the team also remote dual reporting to this HO engineering director, while he or she is based in the Offshore Center).

This HO engineering director will be quite knowledgeable about the projects being executed by his or her HO team and can easily recruit, build, and manage teams in the Offshore Center for executing extensions of these projects. However, since the complete product division extension is being set up in the Offshore Center, he or she also needs to build Offshore Center teams and transfer projects being executed by other engineering directors in his or her product division in the HO. Thus, in preparation for his or her expatriate assignment, he or she should thoroughly prepare himself or herself on these aspects. He or she must hold multiple and detailed discussions with the other HO engineering directors of his or her product division to gain understanding of their projects and their expectations on the expertise and experience of the Offshore Center teams to be recruited and built for their projects. He or she will then be able to achieve the objective of recruiting and building the most effective engineering teams in the Offshore Center for all the projects of his or her product division.

2. The Offshore Center employees have limited knowledge about the overall project or the product (for which they are executing projects), since they are based at a distance from the core center of activities—the HO. These employees have a number of queries and concerns about their activities that need answers from the right entities in the HO.

Hence, when an expatriate manager visits the Offshore Center, the employees in the center perceive him or her as an interface to *all the entities* in the HO, such as the product management and program management teams and even to external entities related to their projects, such as key customers. They expect the expatriate manager to be virtually a "know-all" person who can answer all their queries on their project/product, or at least get the answers from the right HO entities if he or she does not have the answers.

Thus, in preparation for his or her expatriate assignment, the HO manager must develop close relations with all the major HO entities involved with his or her project/product, such as the product management team, the program management team, etc. He or she should also interact with some key external entities related to the project/product, such as the major customers of the project/product, to share valuable inputs with the Offshore Center team on the key customer requirements and feedback on the project/product.

There is a possibility that the HO manager selected for the expatriate assignment may have been working in a "protected" environment with limited interactions with such entities, since his or her manager (the superior manager in HO to whom this expatriate HO manager reports) might be handling the responsibility of interacting with these entities. In such a scenario, this person must change his or her style of working and should start interacting with these entities to prepare for his or her expatriate assignment. For example, he or she may not be interacting directly with the key customers of his or her project/product, and only his or her manager may be making the customer visits, understanding the customers' requirements/feedback, and then guiding him or her to implement them. He or she should now start accompanying his or her manager on these customer visits, develop relationships with the customers, and gain direct knowledge of customer requirements/feedback. He or she will then be able to properly guide the Offshore Center teams on the customer inputs and answer many of their queries.

3. As discussed in the previous section, as a part of his or her expatriate assignment, the HO manager may need to recruit, lead, motivate, and manage Offshore Center teams. As mentioned in Chapter 4, the work culture and norms within the HO may be quite different from the norms in the country of the Offshore Center. Thus, in preparation for his or her expatriate assignment, the HO manager should learn the Offshore Center's work culture, management practices, employee sensitivities, employee career growth expectations, and other related norms.

He or she can learn these norms from multiple sources, such as by requesting other HO managers who have earlier been on expatriate assignments to the country of the Offshore Center (from the current company or from work earlier from another company) to share their experiences, by having informal discussions with the Offshore Center managers and employees visiting the HO, etc.

In fact, the process of learning about the Offshore Center work culture should continue even after he or she has moved to the Offshore Center as an expatriate. In the early part of his or her expatriate assignment, he or she should explore multiple avenues to enhance his or her knowledge of the local work culture—by learning these aspects from the Offshore Center managers and teams, by joining various management forums in the country of the Offshore Center where he or she can interact with managers from the local industry and can learn from their experiences, by attending local management conferences where managers from local industry share their management practices, leadership, and motivation techniques, etc.

It has been noticed that although expatriate managers are keen to learn the work culture and norms of the country of the Offshore Center, some use inappropriate methods to gain this knowledge. In some cases, these methods may backfire and may even badly impact the reputation of the Offshore Center (see Case Study 11.1).

11.3. Possible Additional Roles Post-Expatriate Assignment

A HO manager who has completed his or her expatriate assignment in the Offshore Center has the benefit of having developed in-depth understanding of both the HO and the Offshore Center entities. Since he or she has been working as a manager in the HO for many years, he or she has the benefit of having developed good relationships with various HO entities, such as product management, program management, and key customers. Since he or she has now also been based in the Offshore Center as an expatriate for a reasonable period, he or she has the additional benefit of having developed an understanding of the expertise, strengths, requirements, expectations, aspirations, concerns, and issues of the Offshore Center teams.

The HO senior management should capitalize on these wide set of strengths of HO managers after they return to the HO after their expatriate assignments. One method of achieving this objective might be by assigning additional roles to these managers that require using their cross-location strengths.

Chapter 3 introduced an additional role for HO managers: being a "project coordinator" for independent Offshore Center projects. The vice president for engineering may decide to run some projects *totally independently* within the

Offshore Center. The entire project team will be based in the Offshore Center under an Offshore Center project manager.

Since the company's product management team and key customers are based in the HO, the distance and time-zone difference between the HO and the Offshore Center makes it difficult for the Offshore Center project manager to interact regularly with these entities for the project. In contrast, HO managers are based in the same location as the product management team and key customers. In Chapter 3 it was suggested that the vice president should utilize these location strengths of HO managers by assigning one of them the role of being the "project coordinator" for this completely offshored independent project.

The project coordinator is the interface between the Offshore Center project manager and team with the HO entities related to the project, such as the product management team and the key customers. As mentioned in Chapter 3, the project coordinator needs to handle a range of activities: working with the product management team and key customers to develop a thorough understanding of the product feature set; working with the product management team and the Offshore Center project manager to decide the scope of the current project release by selecting the subset of high-priority features to be implemented based on the available time and resources for the release; sharing any ongoing project requirement changes information regularly with the Offshore Center team by interfacing with the product management team; understanding project-related requirements of the Offshore Center teams and getting them addressed by the product management team; understanding various concerns and issues of the Offshore Center team and resolving them with the relevant HO entities; etc.

As is clear, the HO manager who is selected for such a project coordinator role must have a good understanding of the requirements of the Offshore Center team and must have close relationships with the HO entities to meet all the above objectives. A HO manager with the experience of having completed an expatriate assignment meets both these objectives and is an ideal candidate for the role. Hence, an additional project coordinator role can be assigned to such a HO manager after his or her expatriate assignment, besides his or her handling his or her usual project management role in the HO.

11.4. Avoiding Some Possible Mistakes in Planning Expatriate Assignments

The success of any expatriate assignment depends on choosing the right HO manager for the job and choosing the right duration for the assignment. Some possible mistakes that companies might make in planning expatriate assignments are the following.

1. The HO manager selected for the expatriate assignment should be aware of the work culture of the country of the Offshore Center. The company HO may have some managers who are natives of the country of the Offshore Center and later made their career in the country of the HO. Sometimes the HO senior management is inclined to believe that it is preferable to give a native of the country of the Offshore Center the expatriate assignment since he or she will be more knowledgeable about the work culture and norms of the Offshore Center. The assumption is that the employees in the Offshore Center are his or her "own people" and that he or she "understands" them well, being a native of the same country.

   However, such an approach is flawed and does not always ensure the success of expatriate assignment for the following reasons.

   - The expatriate manager must be able to transfer knowledge of the complete project/product to the Offshore Center team and must be able to address any of their queries/concerns in this process of knowledge transfer. He or she should be able to ensure that during his or her expatriate assignment period the Offshore Center team is fully initiated into the transferred activity and gains all the expertise required to deliver successfully on the activity.

     All the above requirements suggest that the HO manager selected for the expatriate assignment should be a hands-on core expert on the activity, preferably the person heading that activity in the HO. If the head of the activity cannot go on the expatriate assignment, then the next choice should be the person in the HO who is the most knowledgeable about the activity among all the team members. If neither of these persons is a native of the country of the Offshore Center and the company insists on sending a native on the assignment, then the company will end up sending a person who has only a limited role in the activity. Such a person will not be highly knowledgeable about the overall activity. He or she will have only cursory knowledge of most parts of the activity and will be missing the overall picture of the activity. Thus, he or she will fail to transfer the knowledge of the complete activity to the Offshore Center team and will also not be able to address their concerns/queries on the overall activity satisfactorily. The purpose of the expatriate assignment will then not be met as planned.

     The company must realize that knowledge of the Offshore Center work culture is *just one of the expectations* from the expatriate manager and with some effort can be learned within a short time. The core expectation from an expatriate manager is to have deep knowledge of the activity to be transferred and then to transfer the activity successfully to the Offshore Center team. Hence, the company must always select the person with the right expertise for the task, regardless of his or her being a native of any country. Before moving to the Offshore Center, the selected person can prepare himself or herself by learning about the Offshore Center work culture using methods described in Section 11.2.

- Further, the company should not assume that a native of the country of the Offshore Center will necessarily be knowledgeable about the work culture of the country. He or she may have been working in companies in the country of the HO for many years and, hence, may be more attuned to the work culture of the country of the HO than the work culture of the country of the Offshore Center. He or she may then also have to learn about the work culture of the Offshore Center before leaving for the assignment, in the same way as a non-native. Sending such a person may not necessarily produce a positive result unless he or she is truly an expert in the activity being transferred (see Case Study 11.1).

2. As discussed in Section 11.1, some expatriate assignments require the HO manager to set up a division in the Offshore Center and recruit, train, lead, motivate, and manage the team for a limited duration. This HO manager is then supposed to hire a local head for the division, transfer knowledge to him or her, train him or her, and hand over responsibility for heading the Offshore Center division to him or her. The expatriate assignment ends after this limited period.

   However, HO senior management in some companies delay the last task of recruiting a local head (and transferring responsibility to him or her) for a long time, and extend the expatriate assignment period. They let the expatriate manager stay in the Offshore Center and keep managing the local team. The reason for such a decision is usually that the HO senior management believes the expatriate manager is highly knowledgeable about the activity transferred to the Offshore Center, since he or she has years of experience in managing a similar activity in the HO. The HO senior management notices that he or she is managing the Offshore Center team and project quite well, and they fear that any change of leadership to a new local head may impact the project deliverables, since the local head would be new to the domain of the project. Thus, the expatriate manager stays longer on this assignment.

   However, such an approach is flawed, since the core value-add that results from sending the HO manager on the expatriate assignment was for him or her to transfer the extensive knowledge he or she has gained on the projects/product while managing it in the HO. After he or she has transferred the requisite knowledge and has built/trained the Offshore Center team, he or she is then simply managing the team there. He or she is then performing *exactly the same tasks* of leading, motivating, and managing a team as an Offshore Center manager does. The company is then getting no extra value-added from his or her presence, but he or she is still being paid "expatriate manager salary," which is equivalent to his or her HO salary with some additional allowances. The salary outflow for the company is much higher than the salary that would be paid to a local Offshore Center manager for the same function, which unnecessarily increases the costs of the company. Thus, the HO senior management must end the expatriate assignment once the predetermined tasks expected from the expatriate manager are completed, and should then hand over the Offshore Center team to a local manager, who will cost much less for performing the same work and having the same responsibilities.

Further, if the expatriate manager overstays, then the local Offshore Center managers will also realize that he or she is getting a much higher salary for exactly the same project management tasks that they are performing. This huge salary mismatch in the Offshore Center will cause resentment among the local managers and will negatively impact their motivation and deliverables. Thus, such a situation must be avoided by limiting the duration of the expatriate assignment.

Case Study 11.1

A U.S. company had set up an Offshore Center in India with the help of some external consultants. It also hired a small team for the Center, who reported directly to the HO management. As the team grew, the company realized that it needed to hire an Offshore Center head. The company top management decided to send a senior HO manager to the Offshore Center on an expatriate assignment to head and run the center. It was decided that the duration of the assignment would be at least two years, and later the company would decide its next steps.

The top management shortlisted some experienced senior managers in the HO for the assignment. They selected one of them for the role because he was originally from India and had worked for some time in the industry in India, before he decided to make a career move to the United States. The top management thought that since he "understood" India, its people, and its work culture, he would be able to lead and manage the Offshore Center team successfully. The person was sent to India for the assignment.

However, the assumption of the top management that his being a native of India made him an expert on the work culture in the industry in India proved to be wrong. The person had left India many years earlier to pursue a career in the United States. He had spent almost all his career working in the industry in the United States and following the U.S. work culture. Further, when he had left India to make a career in the United States, he was just a young engineer and not a manager. He had absolutely no experience in being a manager and managing teams in India. His knowledge of capabilities of teams in India, local work culture, employees' growth aspirations, management practices, and processes was either very limited or was *almost two decades old*.

He tried to apply his limited and outdated India work culture knowledge in running the Offshore Center, but it obviously failed to deliver in the current environment. Hence, his originally being from India had only made him aware of the "culture" of India, such as knowing about popular movies/songs/dances/sports, but not the "work culture" in India.

He soon realized that he lacked knowledge about running a company's Offshore Center and leading teams in India. He decided to interact with heads/senior managers of various other Offshore Centers in India to gain this knowledge.

Although he was heading the Offshore Center, the professionals in the industry in India were unaware that he was on a long-term assignment of two to more years. He decided to misuse this fact and devised a convoluted way of achieving his objective of interacting with, and learning from, senior managers in the industry in India.

He asked the Offshore Center human resources department to announce a fake recruitment of a managing director (head) for the Center, stating that the current expatriate head would be moving back to the United States after hiring this new local head. Senior professionals from the industry applied for the position, and he started conducting *fake interviews* of these candidates, just to learn from their experiences but with absolutely no intent of offering them the (nonexistent) head position.

The interviewees started becoming suspicious about the intentions of the interviewer when they realized that he was asking them only questions such as the following:

- The management practices, processes, work culture, and norms to be followed in the Offshore Center
- The management hierarchy and employee designations to be followed in the Offshore Center
- Names of highly regarded recruiting agencies to be used for hiring talent
- The best PR agency to be used for building the image of the Offshore Center

No questions were being asked that might be used to judge the interviewee's qualifications, personality, expertise, experience, and fit for the job.

The expatriate manager conducted many such interviews, and when he thought that he had gained sufficient knowledge to run the Offshore Center, he got the company to make a public announcement in India that he was being appointed the managing director of the Center on a *long-term* expatriate assignment.

The senior professionals who had been interviewed for the managing director position realized that their interviews for the position had been a waste of time, since no such job position was actually available in the Offshore Center. They vented their anger by discussing this unethical behavior of the company on some well-known discussion forums in which senior professionals in India participated. The credibility of the Offshore Center was seriously damaged, and later it became difficult for it to get senior professionals to apply to it for other senior management roles. Thus, the Offshore Center failed to hire quality experienced professionals, and its delivery capabilities were adversely impacted.

Interestingly, since the expatriate managing director was not aware of the various industry discussion forums in India, he was also not aware of the negative comments about his company appearing in social media, and so he could not offer any response to comments!

Solution

Although the intent of the expatriate Offshore Center head of interacting with heads/senior managers of various other Offshore Centers in India to gain knowledge of the work culture in India was right, the means he adopted was wrong, or even *unethical*. The better option would have been for him to join some CEO forums about Offshore Centers in India, where he could interact with, and learn from, his peer Offshore Center heads about the norms being followed by them in their respective Centers. Some of these Offshore Center heads might even have themselves been U.S. expatriates, and his interactions with them would have revealed to him the core differences they found between the work cultures in India and in the United States.

He should also have participated actively in the meetings of various project management bodies in India (such as the Project Management Institute), have studied local management literature, and have attended local management conferences where speakers share their experiences of leading teams in India. All these actions would have enhanced his knowledge of the work culture, management practices, and leadership techniques being followed by Offshore Center heads and managers in India, and he would have then been able to apply this knowledge in his work.

He should have also worked toward hiring a senior industry professional, with long years of experience heading companies and managing large teams in India, as the local head for the Offshore Center. He should then have transferred all the company-related knowledge to this local head. He would then have been able to give control of the Center to this local head and return from his expatriate assignment, without the need to stay for a long period of time. Such an experienced and strong local professional would then have been able to implement the local work culture and norms in the Offshore Center and would have been able to run the center successfully.

* * * * *

A number of companies are running their Offshore Centers purely to execute their engineering projects. Hence, value added by their Offshore Centers is still limited. Most of the strategic functions of these companies are still being performed by the HO. Chapter 12 will describe various ways to significantly expand the role of the Offshore Center by making it perform strategic functions for the company—conceiving new products to be developed to increase the company's revenues; deciding new technology and business domains in which to carry out services projects, to win new high-revenue-generating services projects; and making strategic acquisitions to make the Offshore Center team grow significantly, leading to much higher revenues and cost savings for the company. If the Offshore Center makes such strategic contributions, then the company's top management will perceive it to be as highly important and critical to the company as the HO is.

Chapter 12

Using the Offshore Center to Make Strategic Contributions to the Company

Global companies have been running Offshore Centers for many years. However, the role of the Offshore Centers has been mostly limited to handling engineering functions of executing projects. Although companies have been increasing the size of their team in their Offshore Centers, value added by the Offshore Centers to companies has still been limited, primarily because of their limited role. Most of the strategic functions of companies are still being performed by the head office (HO). The HO decides the products to be developed by the company (for product development companies), the business and technology domains in which the company will execute services projects (for services companies), the strategic acquisitions to be made by the company, etc. The Offshore Center has limited, if any, role to play in these strategic functions.

If Offshore Centers are to significantly increase their contribution to their companies' revenues, they should do more than handling plain engineering functions. This chapter questions the assumption that company's strategic functions can necessarily be performed only from the HO. The chapter suggests techniques that will allow the Offshore Centers to *rise to the next level* by performing key strategic functions of the company, despite being at a distance from the HO. This diversification of the functions of the Offshore Center will allow the Offshore Center teams to significantly increase the revenues of the company, significantly reduce the costs of the company, increase the size of the Offshore Center team, and create many more new avenues of career growth for the Offshore Center employees.

If the Offshore Center makes such major strategic contributions to the company, then the company's top management will perceive the Center to be as highly critical and important to the company as the HO is. Thus, in effect, it will be comparable to achieving the "Holy Grail" for any Offshore Center.

The chapter starts by describing the need for involving the Offshore Center head and senior management in the company's strategic decision making. It then describes various ways in which this involvement of the Offshore Center in strategic functions can add significant value to the company—by conceiving new products to be developed to increase company's revenues, by winning high-revenue-generating services business in new technology and business domains, and by allowing the Offshore Center team to grow to a large size through strategic acquisitions, leading to much higher revenues and cost savings for the company.

12.1. Need to Involve the Offshore Center in Strategic Decision Making

The role of the Offshore Center head and the senior management in a company's strategic decision making is generally limited. In some companies, the Offshore Center head is not even considered to be a part of the company's top/senior management responsible for making strategic decisions. He or she is many layers below in the company's global senior management ladder, and the interests of the Offshore Center are represented by a HO senior management person in the strategic management meetings. Once the strategic decisions about the Offshore Center have been made, these decisions are conveyed to the Offshore Center head, for him or her to implement them in the center.

Such an approach is flawed and is not in the interest of the Offshore Center or the company. The Offshore Center head is the most knowledgeable person about the expertise and experience of the Offshore Center team. If he or she is involved in the strategic meetings to decide the projects to be offloaded to the Offshore Center, then he or she can highlight the strengths of his or her team to win large and complex projects for the center. If he or she is not part of the decision-making meetings, the HO senior management will not be able to learn about the strengths of the Offshore Center team in executing large and complex projects and may then offshore only simple and small projects. Thus, the Offshore Center team will not grow to a large size. The contributions of the Offshore Center to the company will be limited, and the company will not achieve high cost savings from offshoring.

Thus, the Offshore Center head must be made a part of the company's global senior management team that makes strategic decisions of the company. Some companies have met this objective by designating their Offshore Center heads at the vice president level in the global top management hierarchy, which makes them a part of the global senior management team. Such a role allows the Offshore Center head to capitalize on the strengths of the Offshore Center to convince the company top management to significantly grow the size of the Offshore Center.

Although, in such companies, the Offshore Center head is considered a part of the global strategic management team, he or she is generally involved only in the strategic decisions that *directly concern the Offshore Center*—such as the type and size of projects to be offloaded to the Offshore Center, the planned growth of the Offshore Center team size, etc. He or she is still not involved in making strategic decisions of the *company as a whole*—such as new products to be developed, new business/technology domains to be entered to win service projects, small companies to be acquired to achieve growth, etc.

In contrast, the HO vice presidents/senior management personnel on these strategic management committees are involved in making all these company-wide strategic decisions. The companies should also involve the Offshore Center head in making all company-wide strategic decisions, instead of limiting his or her role only to Offshore Center–related strategies, for the following reasons.

- The Offshore Center head is a highly capable professional with long years of industry experience.
- He or she has a critical role in the company by virtue of his or her controlling a large part of the company's global team, as the head of the Offshore Center.
- He or she has experience running companies in the past, where he or she made multiple strategic decisions.
- He or she has in the past headed large teams for developing products/ executing services projects.
- He or she has deep knowledge of the expertise and strengths of various competing companies and acquisition targets.

Thus, the Offshore Center head has the requisite knowledge, expertise, and experience to make company-wide strategic decisions, and the company must capitalize on his or her strengths by including him or her in strategic decision making.

He or she can then work closely with the company's top/senior management to make various strategic decisions regarding the company's future products, services project domains, acquisitions, etc. The new projects arising from these decisions can then be executed in the Offshore Center, allowing the center to grow to a much larger size. Further, the Offshore Center can then also start handling a number of strategic responsibilities (such as product management roles) and can add significant value to the company, beyond handling typical engineering project execution responsibilities.

It should be noted that since the Offshore Center head would now be responsible for *company-wide decisions,* some of the projects arising from his or her involvement in these strategic decisions can even be *implemented in the HO.* Thus, his or her strategic role would now be truly global in nature and not limited to the Offshore Center alone.

Besides involving the Offshore Center head in the company's strategic decision making, the company should also include highly capable and senior Offshore Center employees in respective strategic committees for which they have the requisite expertise. For example, Chapter 5 mentioned that senior and capable Offshore Center professionals should be allowed to grow to global top positions and should participate in company-wide strategic decision making. The chapter gave an example of senior technical professionals from the Offshore Center reaching the highest-level technology committee of the company—the "Fellows" committee. Inclusion of such capable Offshore Center professionals in such a committee will allow the committee to make the right technical strategies for the company, which can keep the company ahead of the competition and add significantly to its revenues.

12.2. Conceiving New Products to Be Developed

The key reason for the product management of any company residing within its HO is that the major customers of the products are based in the country of the HO. The product management team needs to be located close to these customers to understand their product requirements and, hence, is based in the HO.

However, product requirements and usage behaviors of customers can vary in different types of geographies. In such scenarios, different kinds of products are required for different geographies. The Offshore Center is located in a different country from the country of the HO. The customer requirements in these two countries can be quite different. Further, customers in a number of other geographies may have similar product requirements and usage behaviors as the customers in the country of the Offshore Center. These geographies require different kinds of products than the products currently being conceived by the

HO product management, which cater to the country of the HO and other similar geographies.

The company should tap the markets in the country of the Offshore Center, and other geographies with similar customer requirements, by developing new products as per requirements of the customers in the country. The Offshore Center team has the advantage of being close to the customers in its country and can understand their requirements to conceive such new products, which will also find markets in other similar geographies.

The company should achieve this objective by setting up a product management team in the Offshore Center. The team will interact closely with key customers in their country to understand their requirements to forecast, strategize, plan, and devise new products for the company. The existing HO product management will not be able to conceive such products, since their focus is on devising products that meet the requirements of a different kind of geography—that of the country of the HO and countries with customers having similar product usage behaviors. The new products conceived by the Offshore Center will find large markets in a range of geographies in which the company had so far not had much success. Thus, the Offshore Center would now be responsible for generating large additional revenues for the company. The company's global top management will then perceive the Offshore Center as being much more critical to the company than being purely a low-cost engineering project implementation center.

Further, the core reason for the company's engineering projects to develop products being mostly controlled from the HO is that the engineering teams in the HO are co-located with the product management team, and also have access to key customers based in the country of the HO. The HO then distributes some modules of these projects to the Offshore Center, with the core modules of the projects still being executed by the HO engineering teams. Thus, the cost savings from offshoring are limited.

Once the Offshore Center team sets up its own product management team and decides to develop products for customers in its country, then the Offshore Center engineering teams will have access to both the product management team and the customers. Such a product can now be developed *totally* within the Offshore Center—starting from deciding the product specifications, to architecture/design, to the final implementation. Thus, the complete engineering team for executing the project will now reside in the low-cost Offshore Center, without the need to have part of the team in the high-cost HO location. The cost savings from offshoring are then significantly higher for the company.

Besides conceiving products for geographies similar to the country of the Offshore Center, its product management should also conceive products that are acceptable *across the globe*. For this purpose, the Offshore Center also needs to have access to key customers in the HO to be able to understand their product requirements, which also reflect the requirements of other geographies with similar customer requirements. This objective should be met by placing some members of the Offshore Center product management team in the HO on long-term expatriate assignments (on a rotation basis). These expatriate product management team members will interact regularly with the key customers in the country of the HO, understand their requirements, and decide new product specifications based on this understanding. Their counterpart product management team members in the Offshore Center will gather requirements from such products from the key customers in the country of the Offshore Center and enhance the product specifications with these inputs. Thus, the products so developed will be truly global in nature, will satisfy requirements of customers across most geographies, will find markets across the globe, and will generate high revenues for the company. The engineering project for developing such a global product can be distributed across the HO and the Offshore Center, with each location implementing project modules for the specifications generated from the requirements of key customers within its own country.

This strategy of adding the additional domain of product management functions to the Offshore Center will also result in multiple benefits for the employees of the Center.

1. Instead of the Offshore Center having only the engineering domain, it will now offer additional domains of work. The employees will have options for lateral career movement to different domains of work. Interested employees will achieve more job satisfaction, since they will be working in new exciting domains of work, rather than being limited to a single domain. They will be learning new skills and dealing with new challenges, which will result in improving their motivation, productivity, and retention. Further, addition of more domains of work will also generate more opportunities for career growth within the Offshore Center for the employees.

2. Chapter 5 mentioned that a major reason that prevents senior and capable Offshore Center employees from reaching global top positions of the company is their limited knowledge and exposure, since the role of the Offshore Center is limited primarily to implementing engineering projects controlled mostly from the HO. Companies expect their top management and technical personnel to have detailed understanding of the company's markets, requirements of key customers, product management strategies, etc. Since the Offshore Center employees lack such exposure, they are generally not considered for promotions to global top positions.

   Once the Offshore Center establishes its own product management function and starts developing products with input from key local customers, then its senior employees will have similar exposure to these entities, comparable to that of their HO counterparts. These senior Offshore Center employees will then have greater exposure to the markets, customers, and product management, and will be considered suitable for promotions to global top positions. Thus, senior Offshore Center employees will see excellent global career growth opportunities, which will not only improve their motivation and productivity but will also motivate the rest of the Offshore Center team to perform beyond their potential to reach such top positions.

Further, the company will then have only the most capable and deserving professionals at its global top management and technical positions, unconstrained by the location of work of these professionals. Such a strong top leadership team will then decide and implement the right strategies to take the company to new heights, in terms of achieving significant improvement in revenues, profits, and growth.

12.3. Entering New Services Domains

Many services companies are running Offshore Centers. Each services company identifies a set of business and technology domains in which it executes projects for its customers. The customers may have requirements for services projects in other domains as well, but the company does not bid for those projects since it lacks expertise in those domains. The company realizes that heavy investment is required to recruit and build teams with expertise in a new domain and, hence, generally avoids such initiatives.

If the Offshore Center head is involved in making strategic decisions of the company, then he or she can tap on the strengths of the Offshore Center team to suggest new domains of expertise in which the company can execute services projects. The Offshore Center will have a large team executing projects in the expertise domains of the company. A number of these employees may also have prior experience executing projects in some other domains in their earlier companies. The Offshore Center head will be aware of these strengths of his or her team. He or she can evaluate various project requirements coming from the company's customers and can identify a set of domains, outside the current expertise domains claimed by the company, for which the maximum project requirements are coming. From these domains, he or she can identify the domain(s) in which a substantial number of Offshore Center employees already have prior experience and expertise. He or she can use this strength of the Offshore Center to convince the company top management to adopt this domain as a new area of expertise of the company to execute services projects. He or she can also share with the top management that a large number of people with expertise in that domain exists in the industry close to the Offshore Center and can be recruited at short notice and at a low cost (compared to the investment required for building a similar team in the HO) if the company ends up receiving multiple large projects in that domain in the near future.

The company can then adopt this new domain, with its team being based in the Offshore Center. The company will then be able to win large and multiple projects in an additional domain, resulting in a significant additional source of revenues for the company. Since these projects will be executed in the Offshore Center, the center will grow to a much larger size, leading to higher cost savings for the company.

12.4. Inorganic Growth through Strategic Acquisitions

The Offshore Center head should also be involved in making decisions of the company on strategic acquisitions of other, smaller companies. If the Offshore Center grows only through organic means, by hiring and building new teams, then growth will be slow because of the long cycle time in recruiting and training individual employees. The company will not be able to win and execute a large number of projects within a short time span, leading to slow revenue growth. Hence, the company should instead look for options for inorganic growth to a large team size by acquiring small companies that have expertise in the domains of work of the company.

The Offshore Center head should be quite knowledgeable about the industry in his or her country. He or she is aware of local companies that possess talent with expertise in the domains of projects of his or her company. He or she is aware of which of these companies are open to being acquired. He or she will establish contacts with such companies, evaluate their expertise, and short-list the right company to be acquired. After performing due diligence, the top management may then decide to acquire the company.

As a result, the company will have a large offshore team spread across the Offshore Center and other acquired companies in the same country, with these acquired companies acting as extensions to the Offshore Center. The Offshore Center head will be the overall head of all these centers. Since the company now has access to a much larger offshore team, it can bid on, win, and execute many more and large projects than it was formerly able to do. Thus, the company can quickly ramp up its revenues in an inorganic fashion. This revenue growth comes coupled with large cost savings, since these projects will be executed in low-cost offshore locations.

As discussed in the previous section, the Offshore Center head will also be aware of some domains in which the company receives a large number of project requirements but is unable to bid because the company lacks expertise in these domains. He or she can decide to acquire local companies with expertise in these domains, to allow the company to obtain expertise in new domains and thus to win many more additional projects.

Finally, the acquired company will also have its own set of existing customers for whom it is executing projects. These customers may have project requirements in a range of domains, but the acquired company will be executing projects only in its own expertise domain. The Offshore Center head will build relationships with these customers, highlight the expertise of his or her company in a range of additional domains, and win additional projects in these domains from these customers. Thus, the company now receives additional sources of revenues from a new set of customers.

Appendix

Abbreviations and Acronyms

ACM	Association for Computing Machinery
CEO	Chief executive officer
CTO	Chief technology officer
HO	Head office
HR	Human resources
IEEE	Institute of Electrical and Electronics Engineers
IPR	Intellectual property rights
KRA	Key result area
MTS	Member technical staff
PMI	Project Management Institute
PR	Public relations
SMTS	Senior member technical staff
VC	Venture capitalist

Index